BUILDING BLOCKS OF ENGLISH

ADVANCED CONSONANTS AND VOWELS

Written by Jeff De La Rosa

Illustrated by Ruth Bennett

a Scott Fetzer company
Chicago

This edition is co-published by agreement between World Book, Inc. and Cherry Lake Publishing Group

World Book, Inc.
180 North LaSalle Street
Suite 900
Chicago, Illinois 60601
USA

Cherry Lake Publishing Group
2395 South Huron Parkway
Suite 200
Ann Arbor, MI 48104
USA

© 2024. All rights reserved. This volume may not be reproduced in whole or in part in any form without prior written permission from the publisher.

WORLD BOOK and the GLOBE DEVICE are registered trademarks or trademarks of World Book, Inc.

WORLD BOOK STAFF

Editorial

Vice President
Tom Evans

Senior Manager, New Content
Jeff De La Rosa

Curriculum Designer
Caroline Davidson

Proofreader
Nathalie Strassheim

Graphics and Design

Senior Visual Communications Designer
Melanie Bender

Library of Congress Control Number: 2024936272

Building Blocks of English
ISBN: 978-0-7166-5517-6 (set, hardcover)

Advanced Consonants and Vowels
ISBN: 978-0-7166-5519-0 (hardcover)

Also available as:
ISBN: 978-0-7166-5529-9 (e-book)

Cherry Lake ISBNs

Building Blocks of English
ISBN: 978-0-7166-8821-1 (set, softcover)

Advanced Consonants and Vowels
ISBN: 978-0-7166-8791-7 (softcover)

Printed in the United States of America

Acknowledgments:
Writer: Jeff De La Rosa
Illustrator: Ruth Bennett/The Bright Agency
Series Advisor: Marjorie Frank

TABLE OF CONTENTS

The Story So Far... 4
The Letter Y 6
Vowel Teams 8
Consonant Blends 14
Consonant Digraphs 18
Syllables 22
Silent Letters 30
The Letter X 34
The Silent E 36
Show What You Know 38
Answers and Words to Know 40

There is a glossary on page 40. Terms defined in the glossary are in type **that looks like this** on their first appearance.

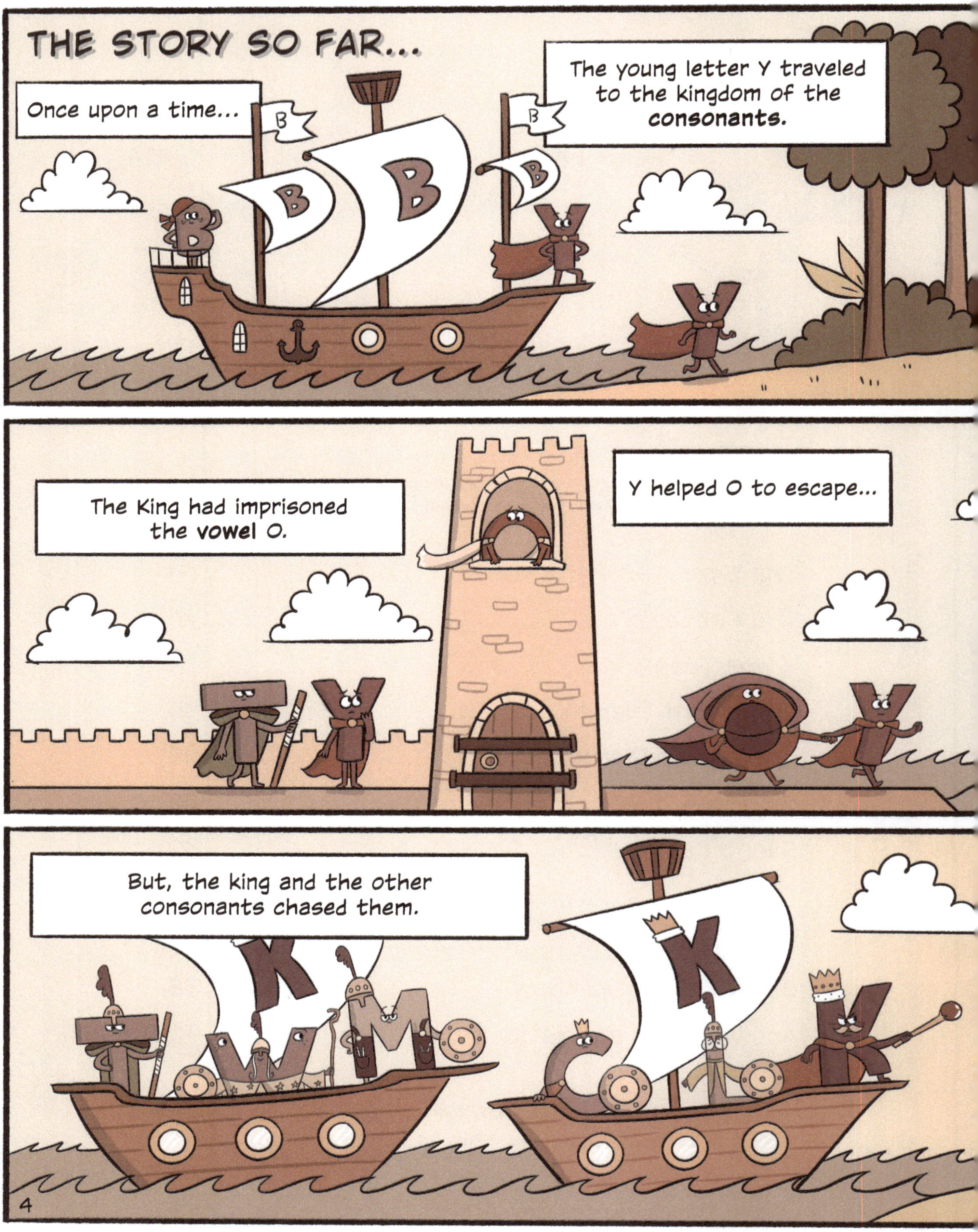
THE STORY SO FAR...
Once upon a time...
The young letter Y traveled to the kingdom of the **consonants.**
The King had imprisoned the **vowel** O.
Y helped O to escape...
But, the king and the other consonants chased them.

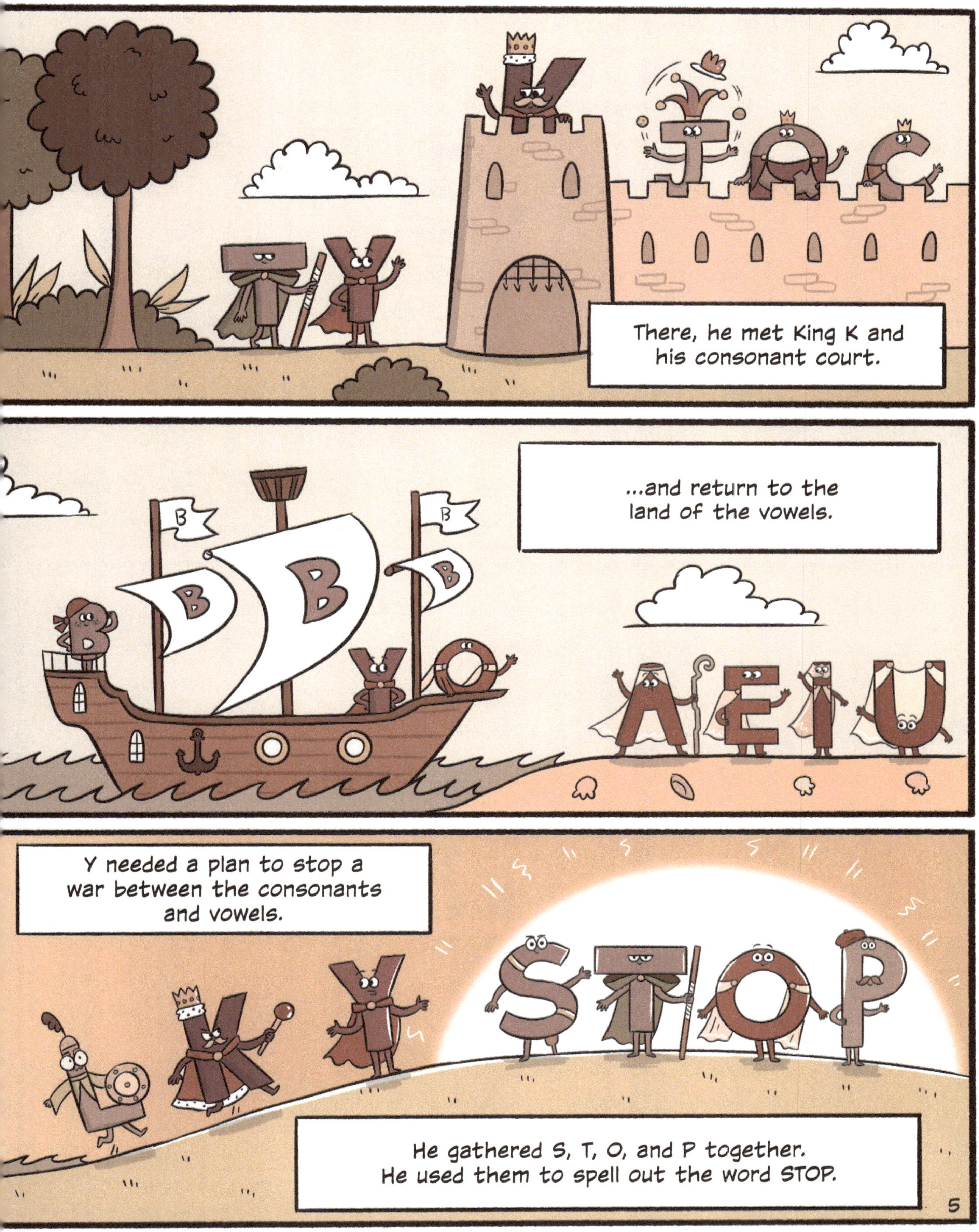
There, he met King K and his consonant court.
...and return to the land of the vowels.
Y needed a plan to stop a war between the consonants and vowels.
He gathered S, T, O, and P together. He used them to spell out the word STOP.

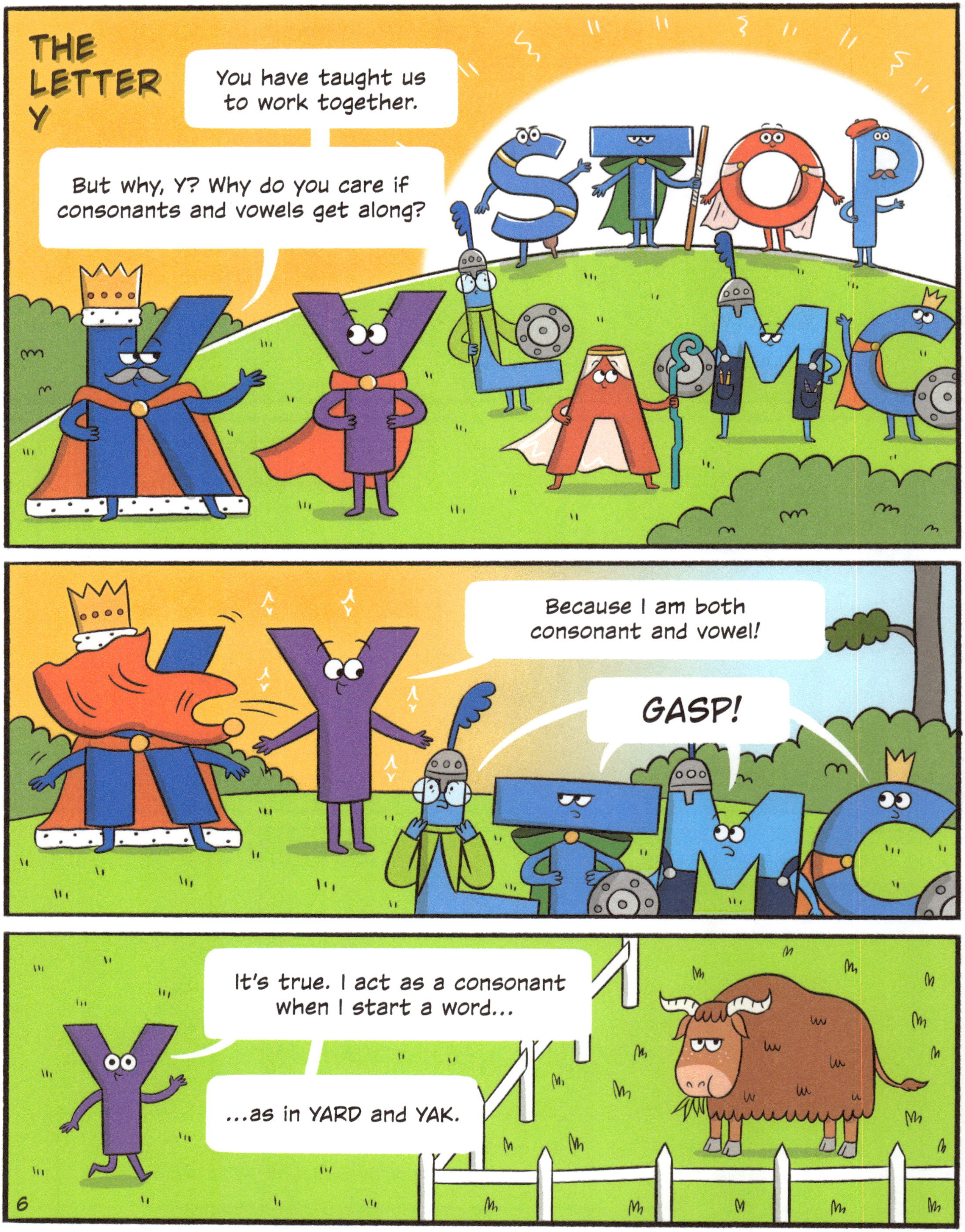

THE LETTER Y
You have taught us to work together.
But why, Y? Why do you care if consonants and vowels get along?
Because I am both consonant and vowel!
GASP!
It's true. I act as a consonant when I start a word...
...as in YARD and YAK.

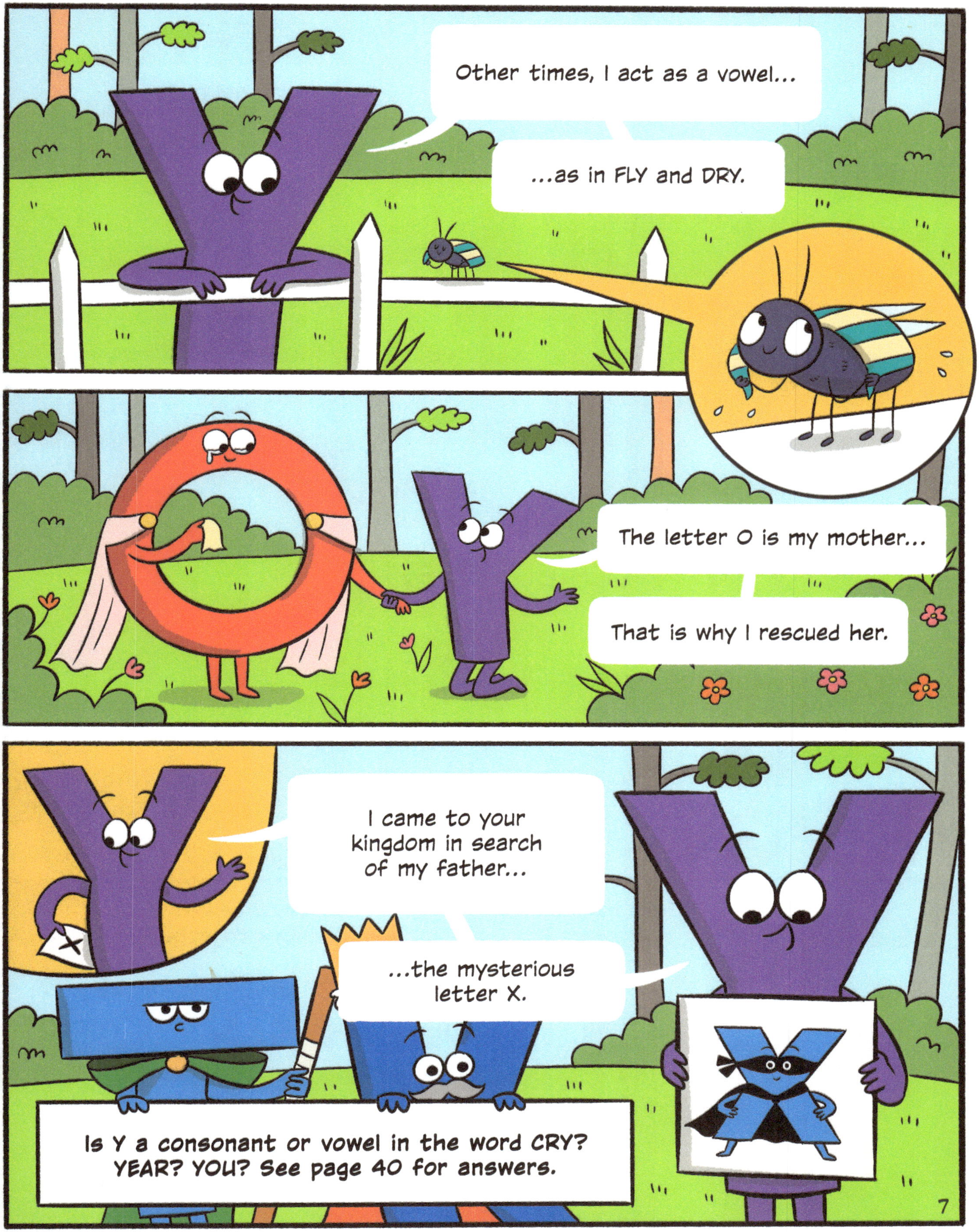
Other times, I act as a vowel...
...as in FLY and DRY.
The letter O is my mother...
That is why I rescued her.
I came to your kingdom in search of my father...
...the mysterious letter X.
Is Y a consonant or vowel in the word CRY? YEAR? YOU? See page 40 for answers.

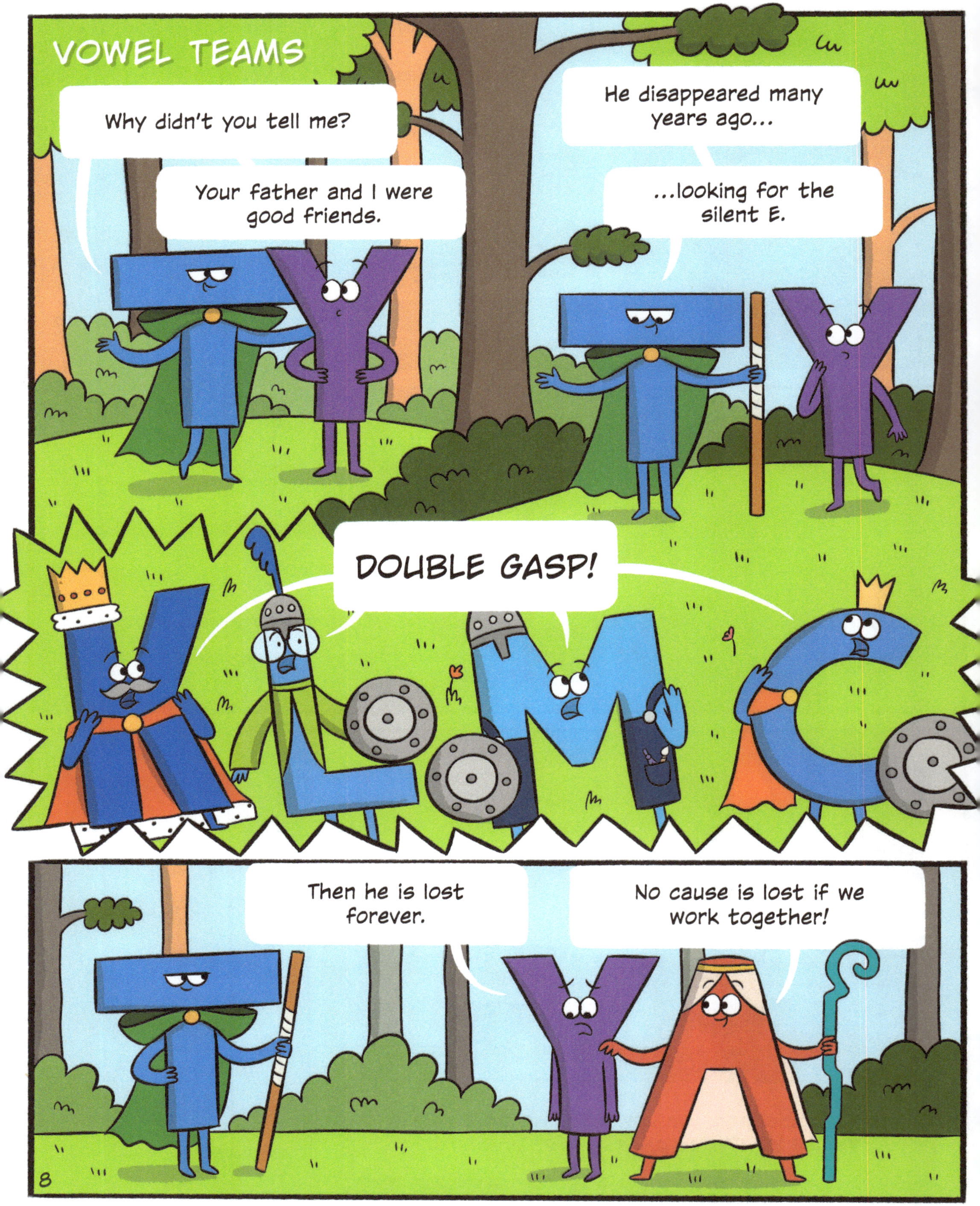
VOWEL TEAMS
Why didn't you tell me?
Your father and I were good friends.
He disappeared many years ago...
...looking for the silent E.
DOUBLE GASP!
Then he is lost forever.
No cause is lost if we work together!

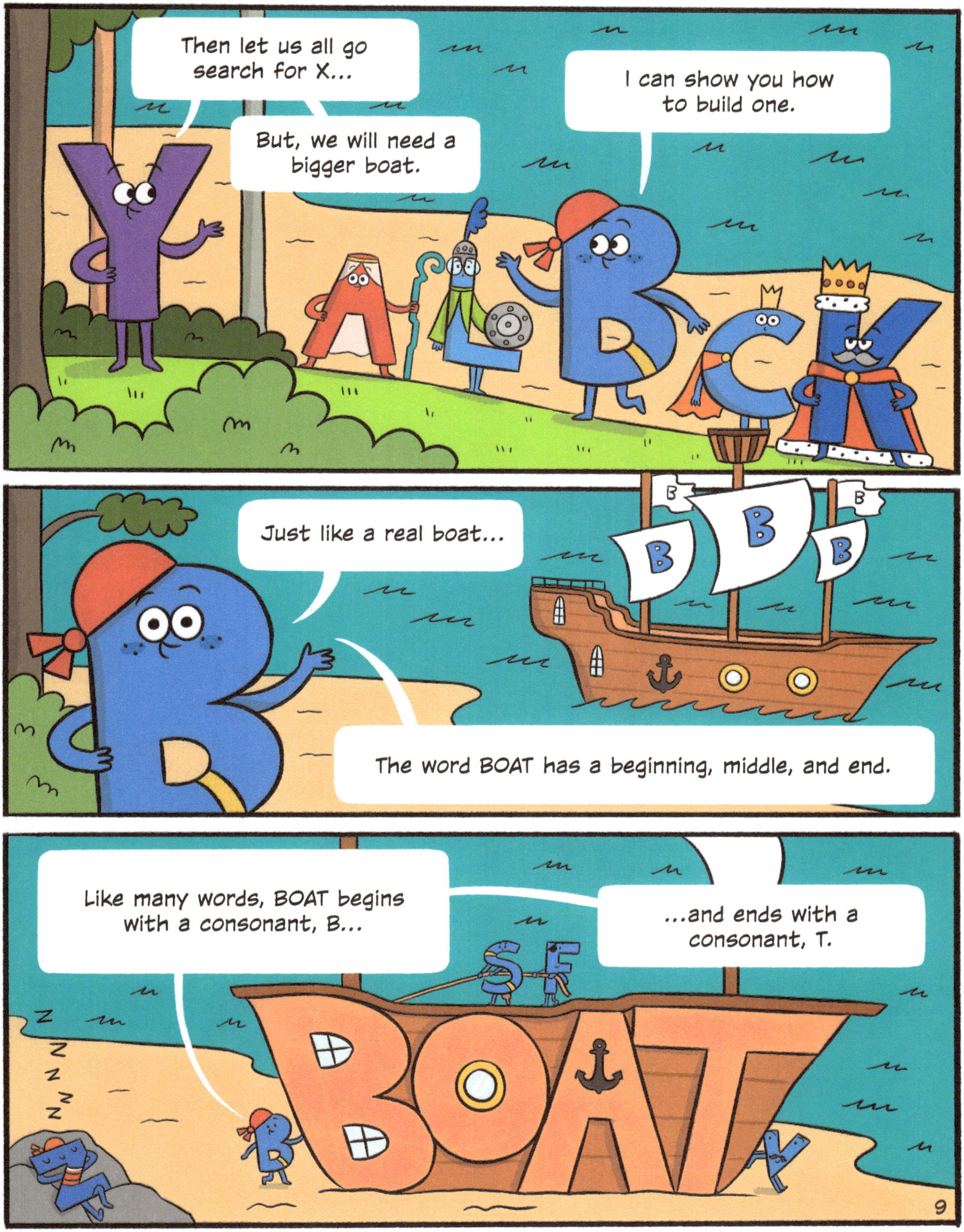

Then let us all go search for X...
But, we will need a bigger boat.
I can show you how to build one.
B
B
B
B
B
Just like a real boat...
The word BOAT has a beginning, middle, and end.
Like many words, BOAT begins with a consonant, B...
...and ends with a consonant, T.
Z
Z
Z
Z
Z
BOAT

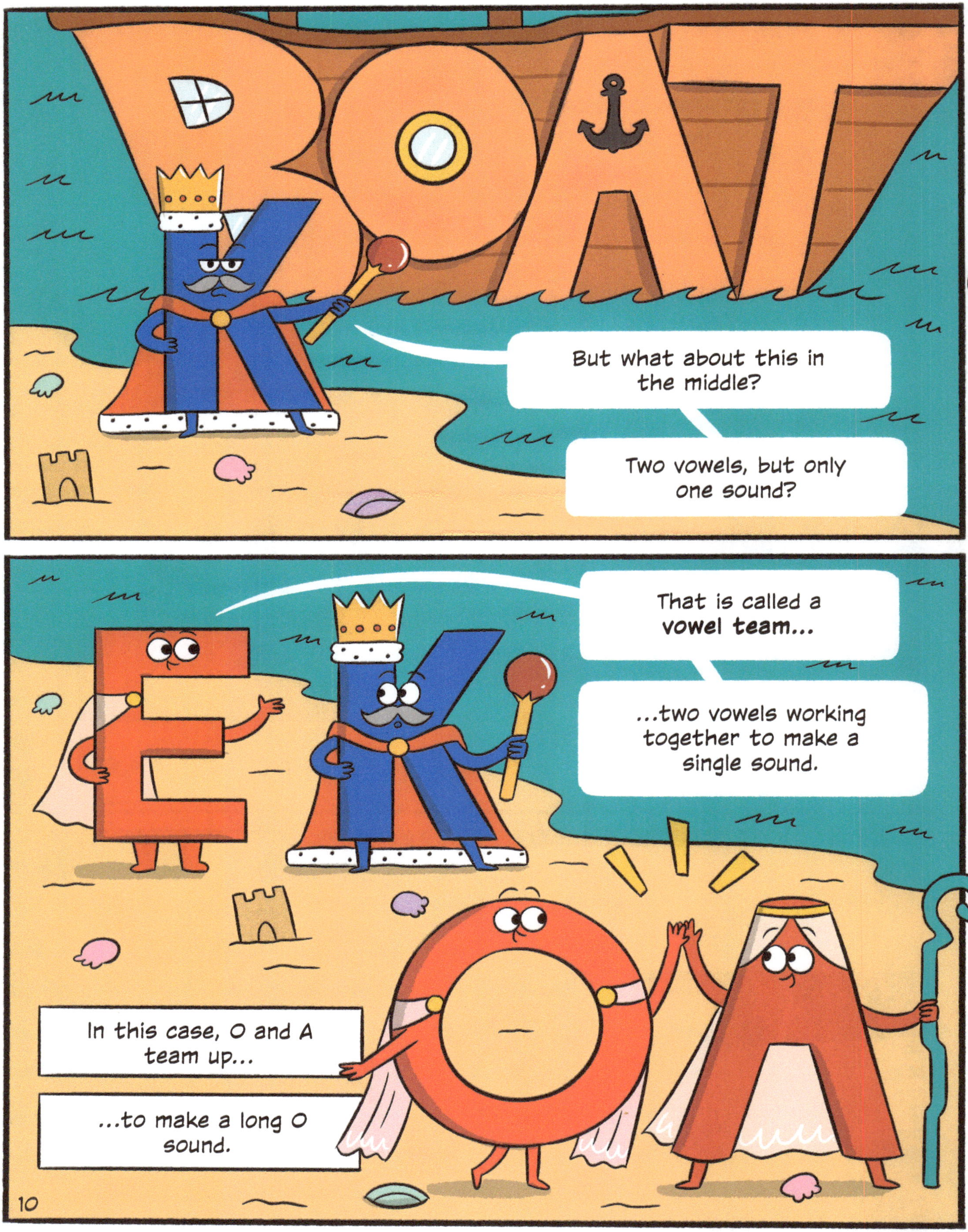

BOAT
But what about this in the middle?
Two vowels, but only one sound?
That is called a **vowel team...**
...two vowels working together to make a single sound.
In this case, O and A team up...
...to make a long O sound.

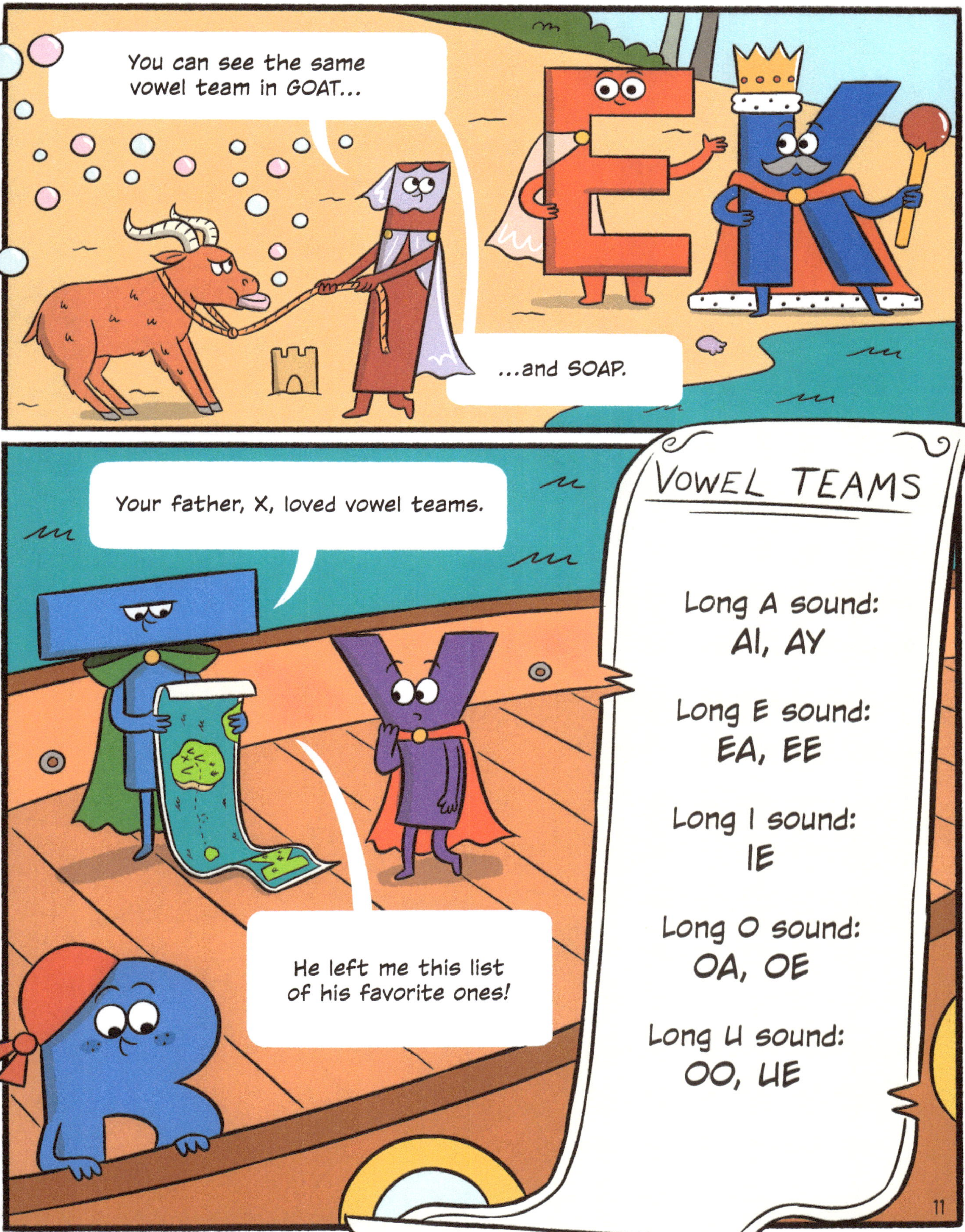

You can see the same vowel team in GOAT...
...and SOAP.
Your father, X, loved vowel teams.
He left me this list of his favorite ones!
VOWEL TEAMS
Long A sound: AI, AY
Long E sound: EA, EE
Long I sound: IE
Long O sound: OA, OE
Long U sound: OO, UE

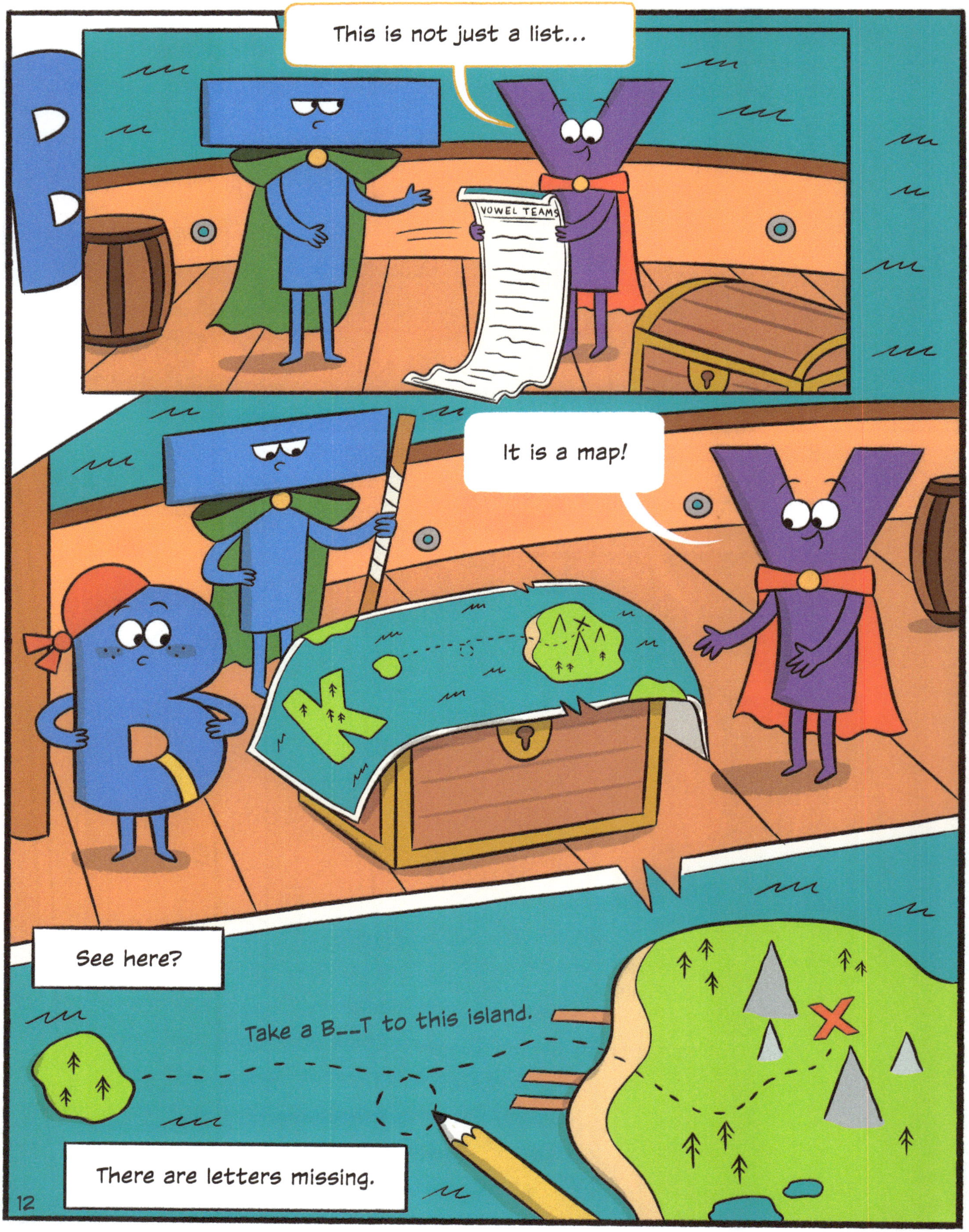
This is not just a list...
VOWEL TEAMS
It is a map!
See here?
Take a B__T to this island.
There are letters missing.

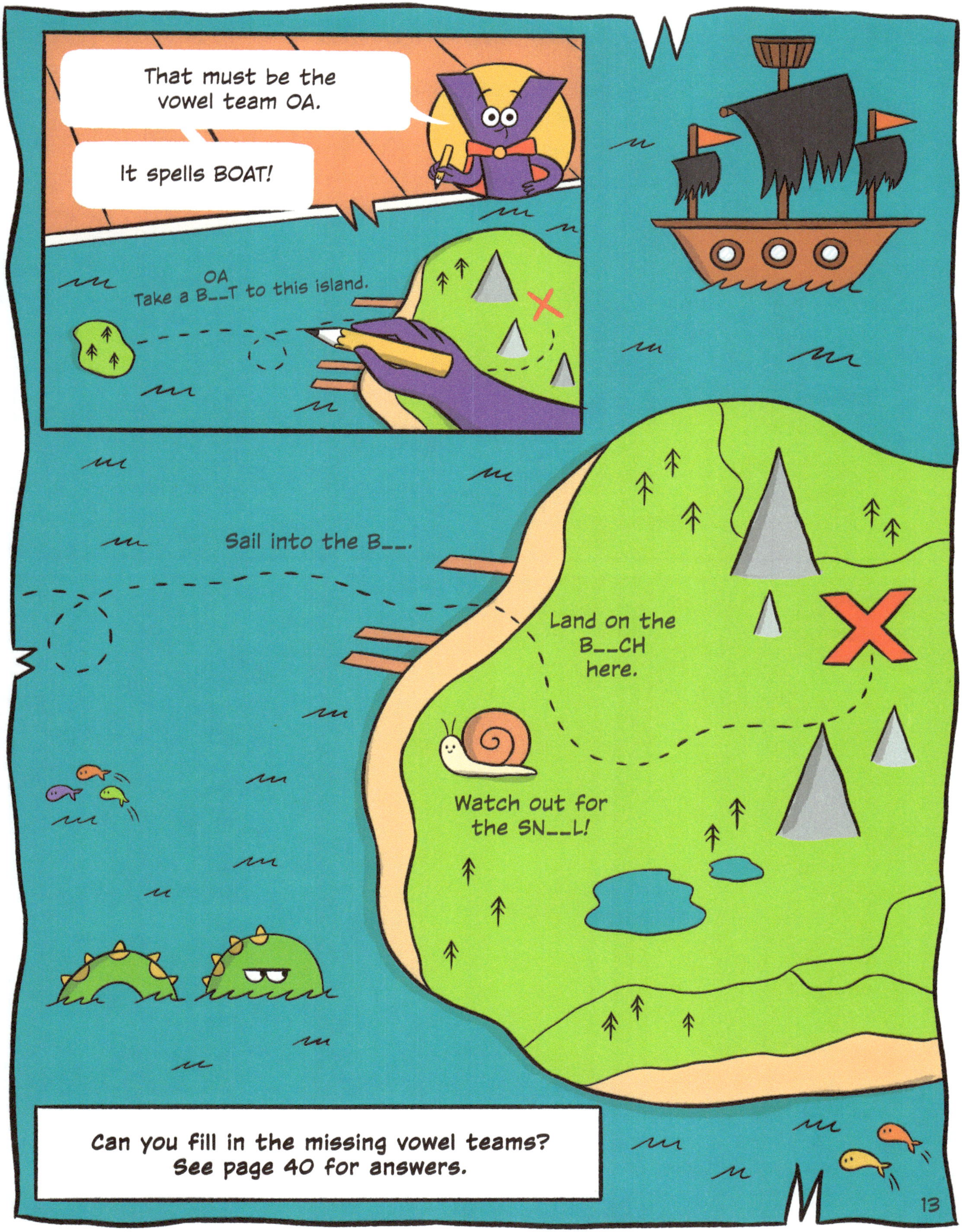
That must be the vowel team OA.
It spells BOAT!
OA
Take a B__T to this island.
Sail into the B__.
Land on the B__CH here.
Watch out for the SN__L!
Can you fill in the missing vowel teams? See page 40 for answers.

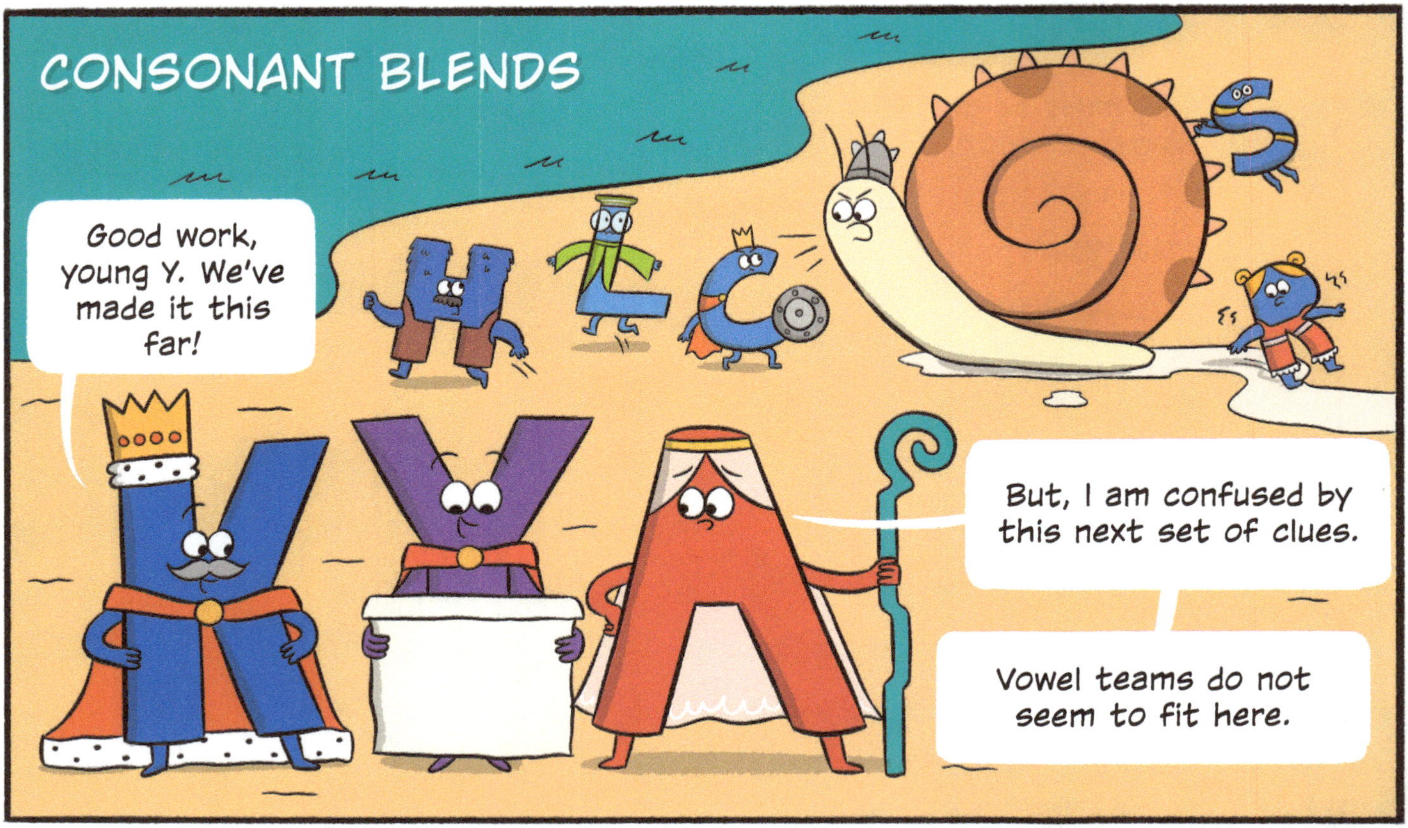
CONSONANT BLENDS
Good work, young Y. We've made it this far!
But, I am confused by this next set of clues.
Vowel teams do not seem to fit here.

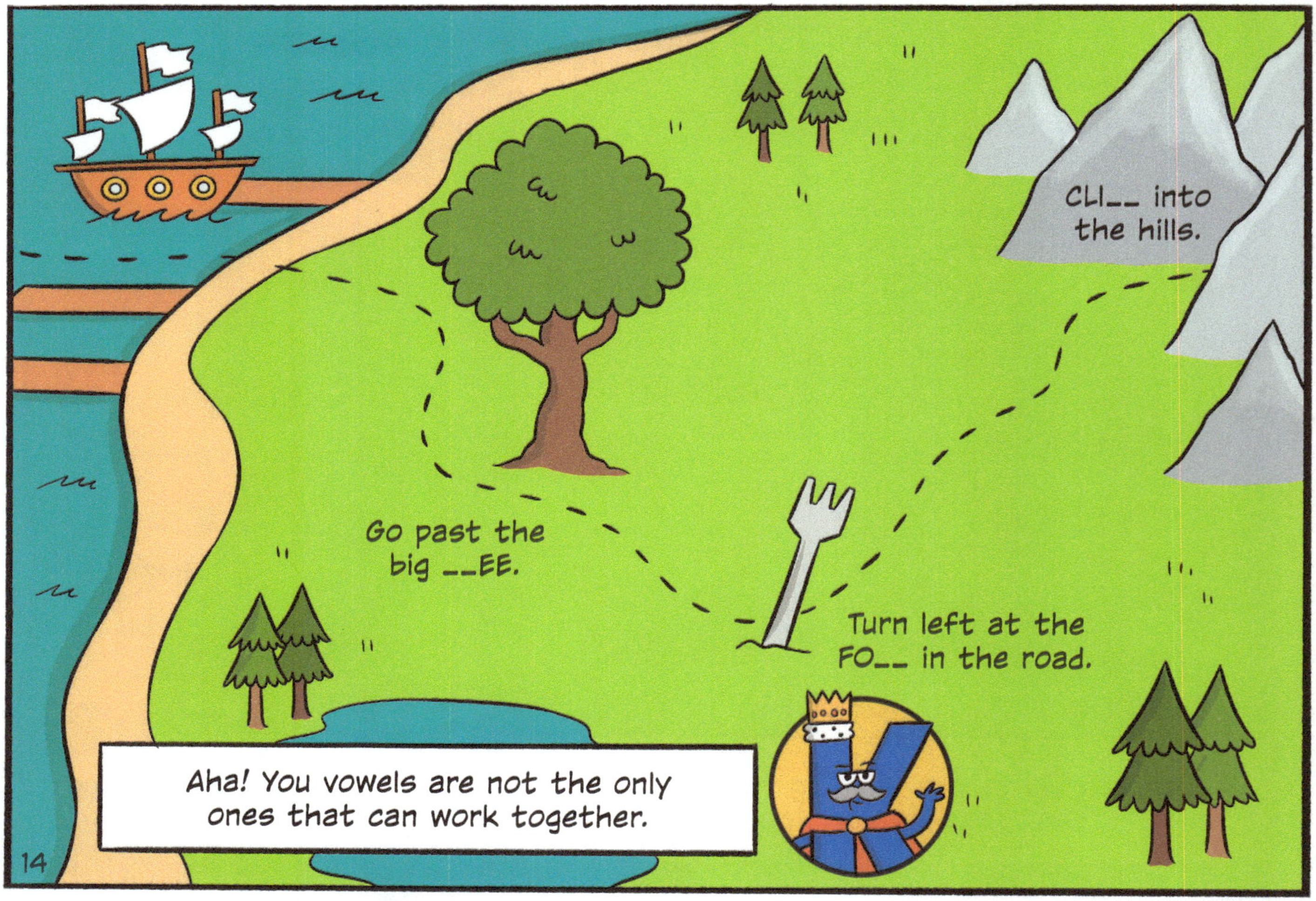
CLI__ into the hills.
Go past the big __EE.
Turn left at the FO__ in the road.
Aha! You vowels are not the only ones that can work together.

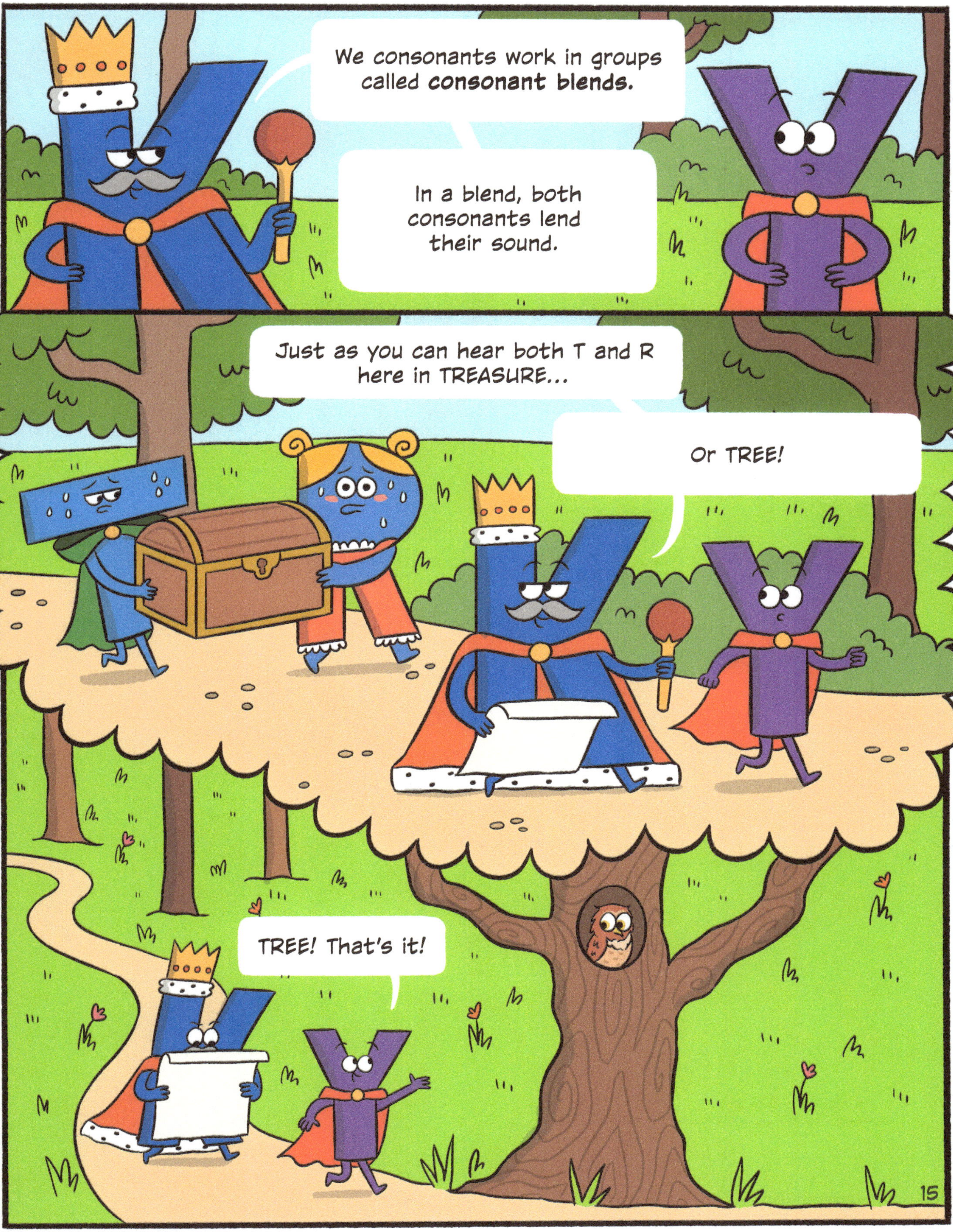

We consonants work in groups called **consonant blends.**
In a blend, both consonants lend their sound.
Just as you can hear both T and R here in TREASURE...
Or TREE!
TREE! That's it!

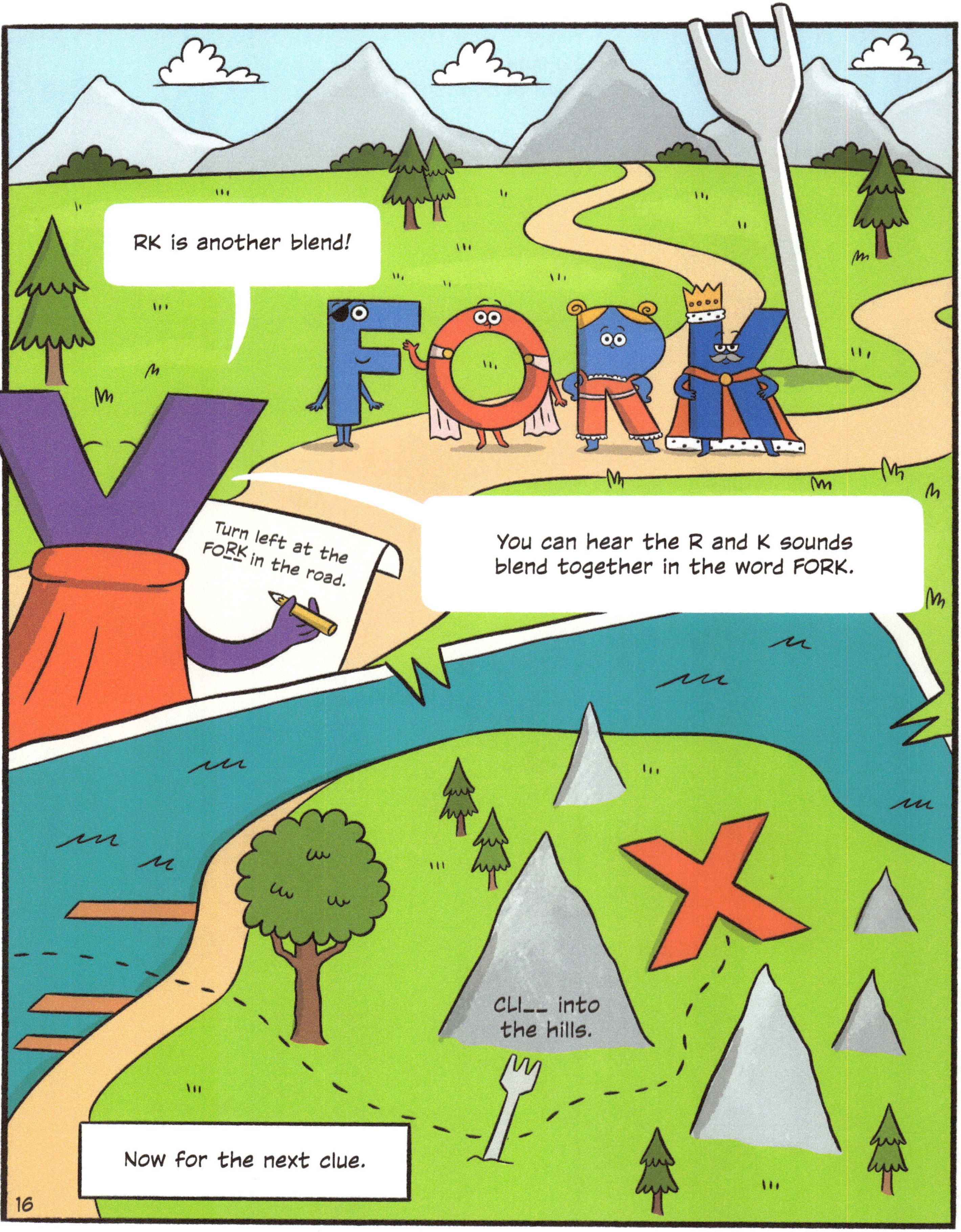

RK is another blend!
Turn left at the FORK in the road.
You can hear the R and K sounds blend together in the word FORK.
Now for the next clue.
CLI__ into the hills.

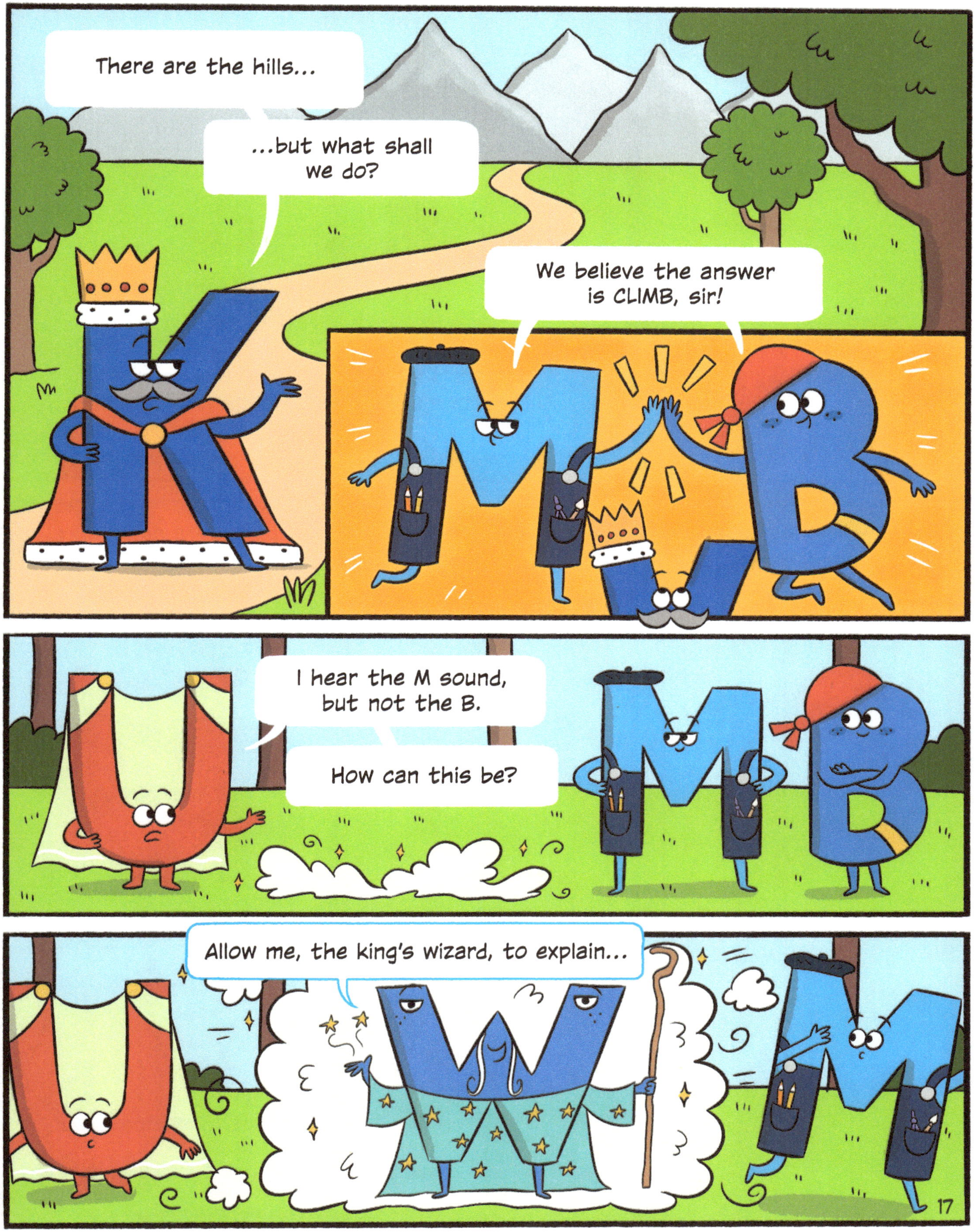
There are the hills...
...but what shall we do?
We believe the answer is CLIMB, sir!
I hear the M sound, but not the B.
How can this be?
Allow me, the king's wizard, to explain...

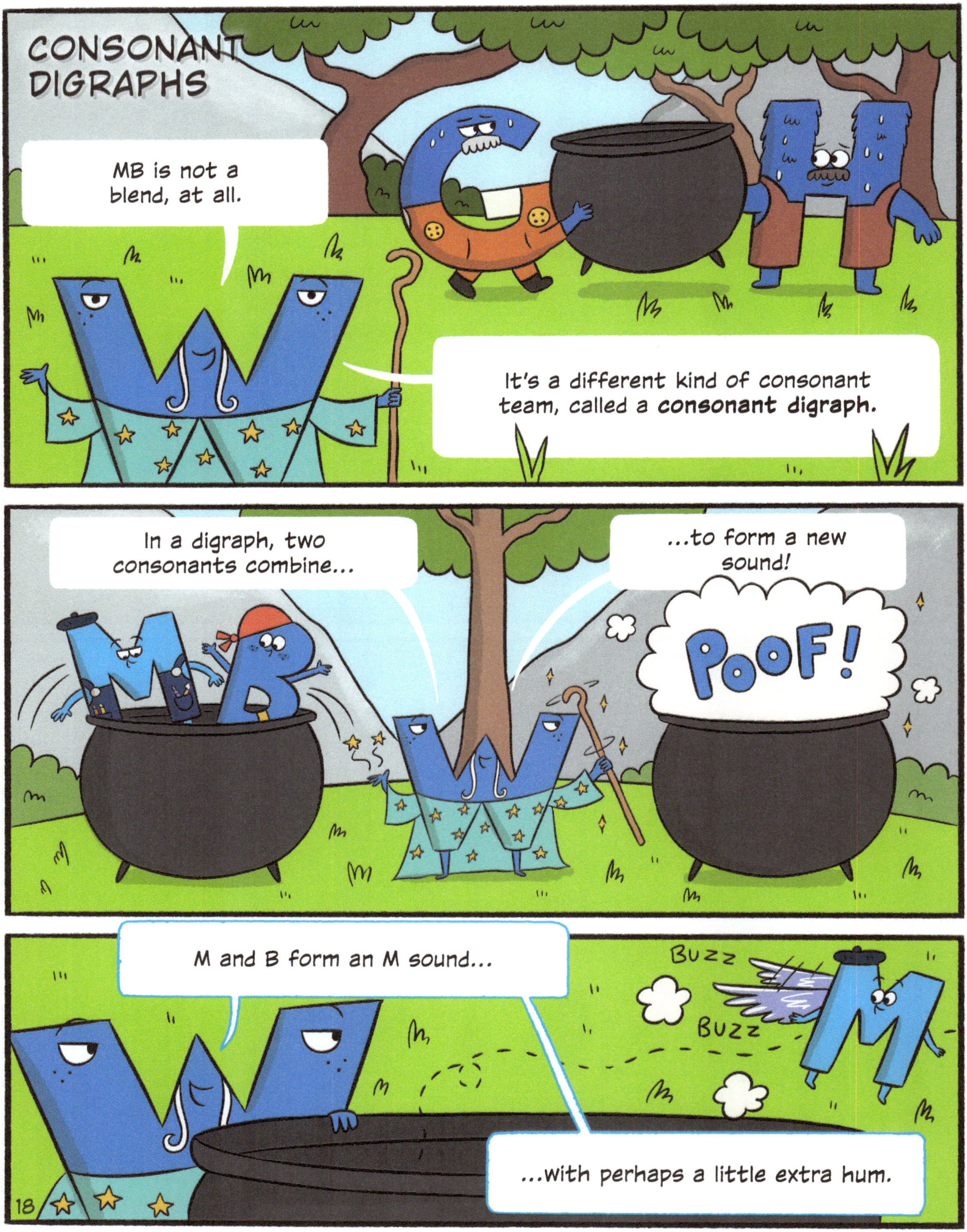
CONSONANT DIGRAPHS
MB is not a blend, at all.
It's a different kind of consonant team, called a **consonant digraph.**
In a digraph, two consonants combine...
...to form a new sound!
POOF!
M and B form an M sound...
BUZZ
BUZZ
...with perhaps a little extra hum.

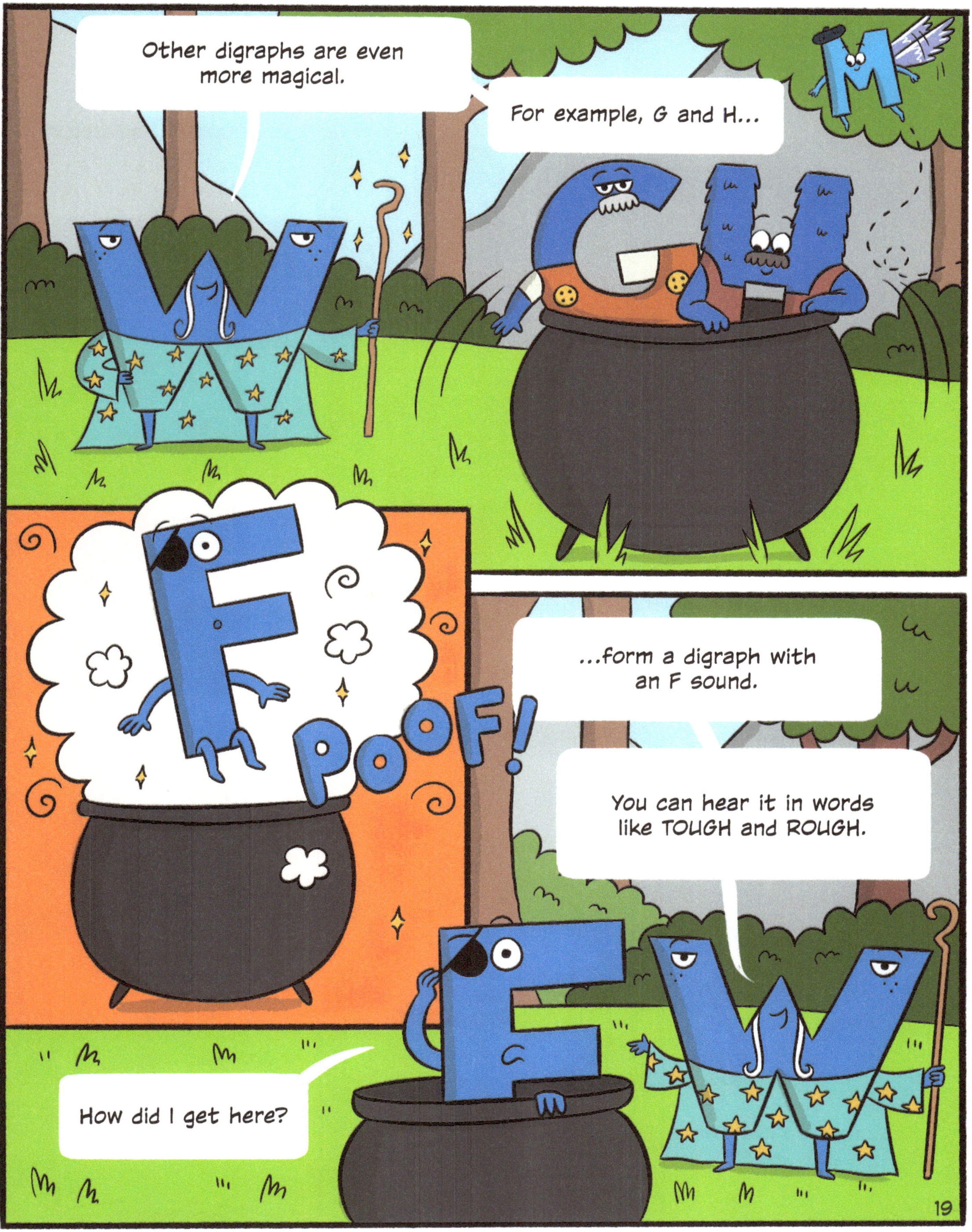
Other digraphs are even more magical.
For example, G and H...
POOF!
...form a digraph with an F sound.
You can hear it in words like TOUGH and ROUGH.
How did I get here?

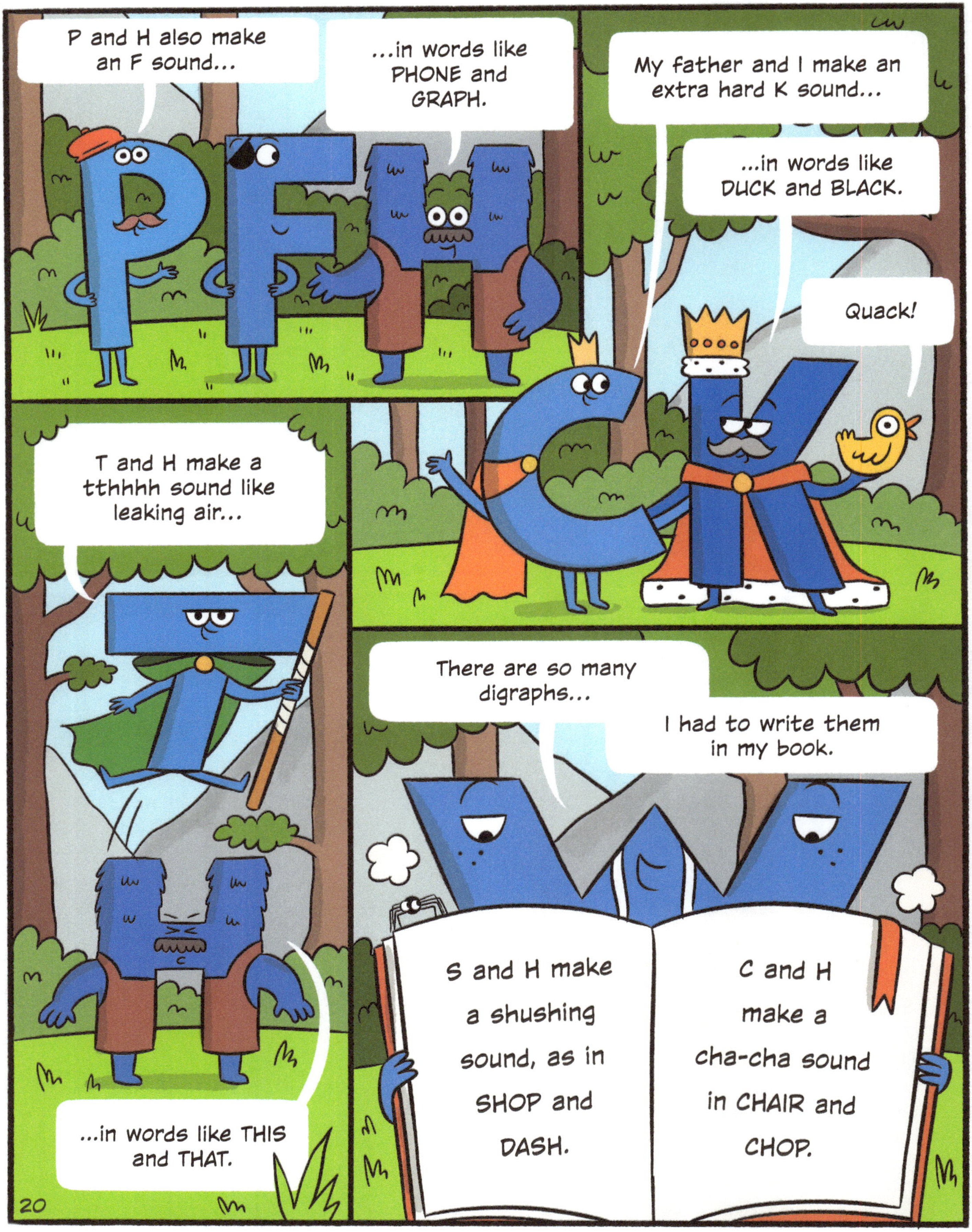
P and H also make an F sound...
...in words like PHONE and GRAPH.
My father and I make an extra hard K sound...
...in words like DUCK and BLACK.
Quack!
T and H make a tthhhh sound like leaking air...
...in words like THIS and THAT.
There are so many digraphs...
I had to write them in my book.
S and H make a shushing sound, as in SHOP and DASH.
C and H make a cha-cha sound in CHAIR and CHOP.

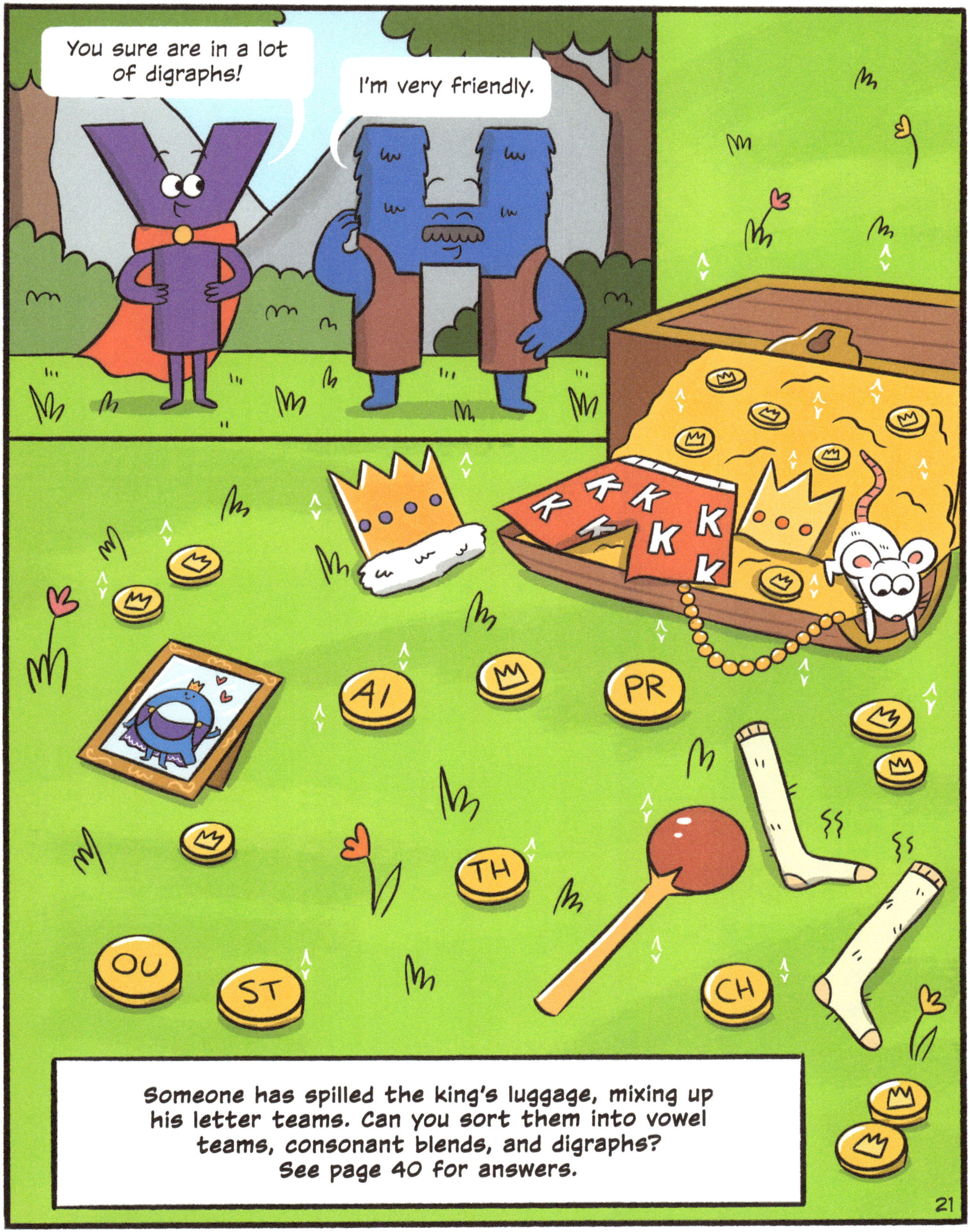
You sure are in a lot of digraphs!
I'm very friendly.
AI
PR
TH
OU
ST
CH
Someone has spilled the king's luggage, mixing up his letter teams. Can you sort them into vowel teams, consonant blends, and digraphs?
See page 40 for answers.

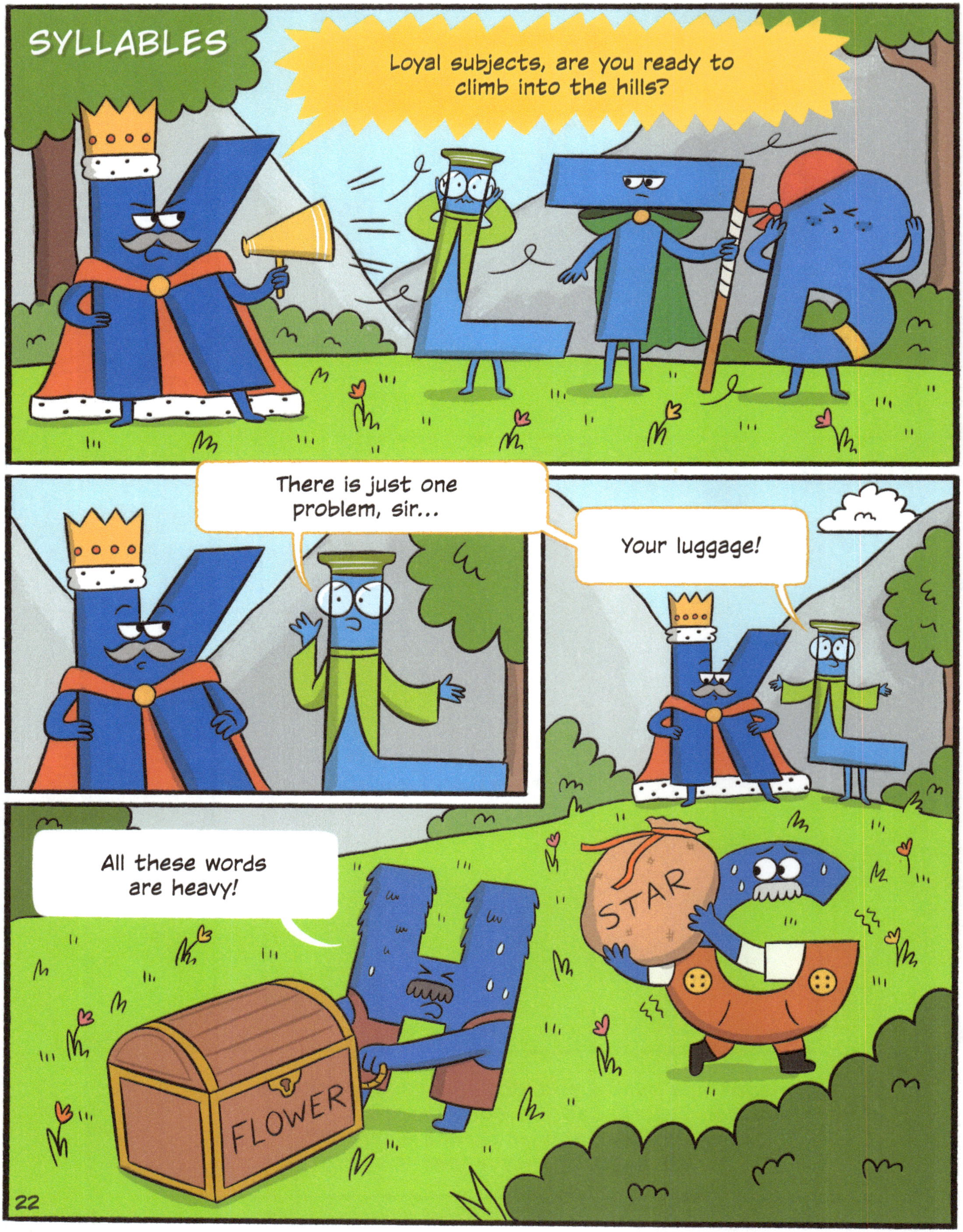
SYLLABLES
Loyal subjects, are you ready to climb into the hills?
There is just one problem, sir...
Your luggage!
All these words are heavy!
STAR
FLOWER

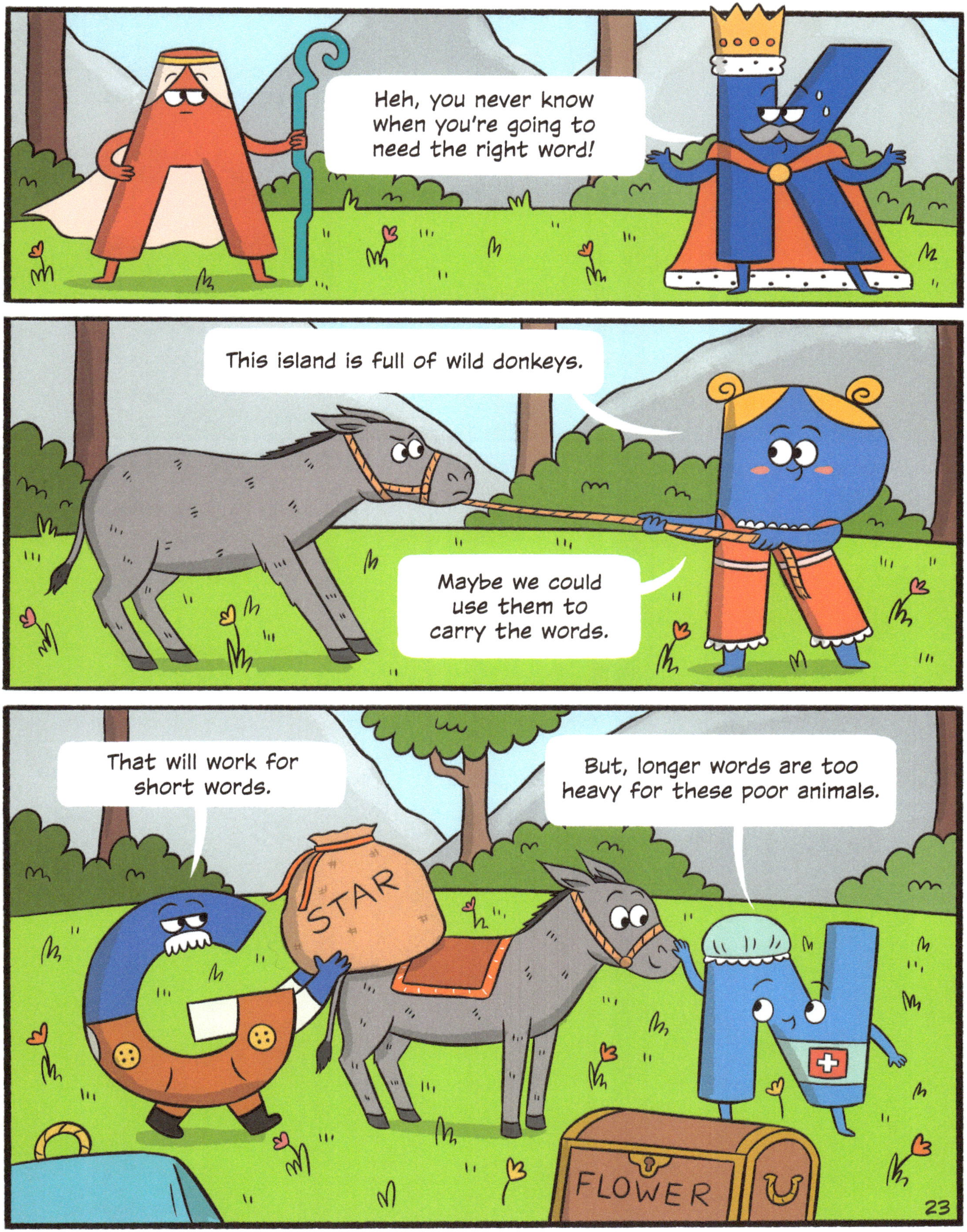
Heh, you never know when you're going to need the right word!
This island is full of wild donkeys.
Maybe we could use them to carry the words.
That will work for short words.
STAR
But, longer words are too heavy for these poor animals.
FLOWER

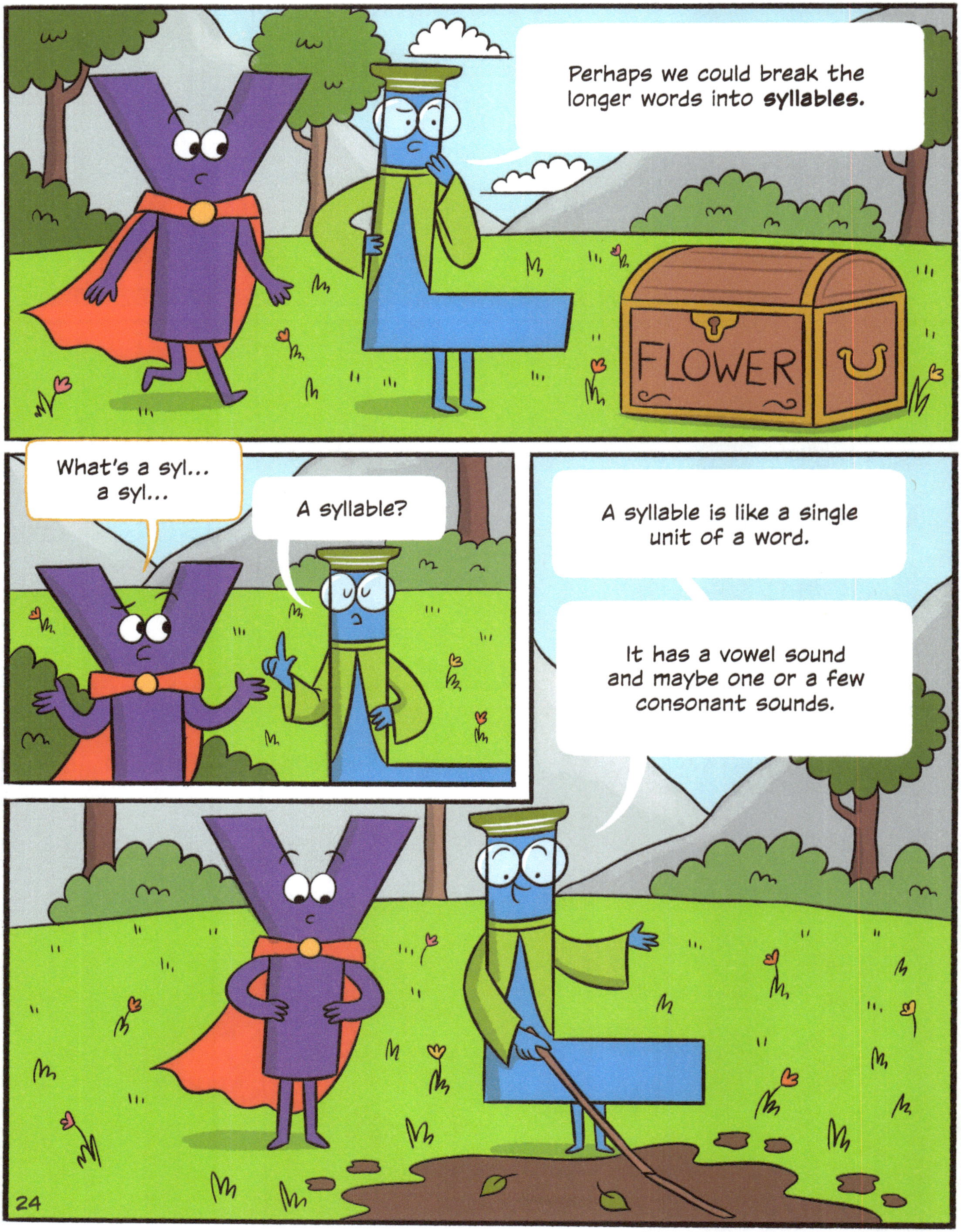
Perhaps we could break the longer words into **syllables.**
FLOWER
What's a syl... a syl...
A syllable?
A syllable is like a single unit of a word.
It has a vowel sound and maybe one or a few consonant sounds.

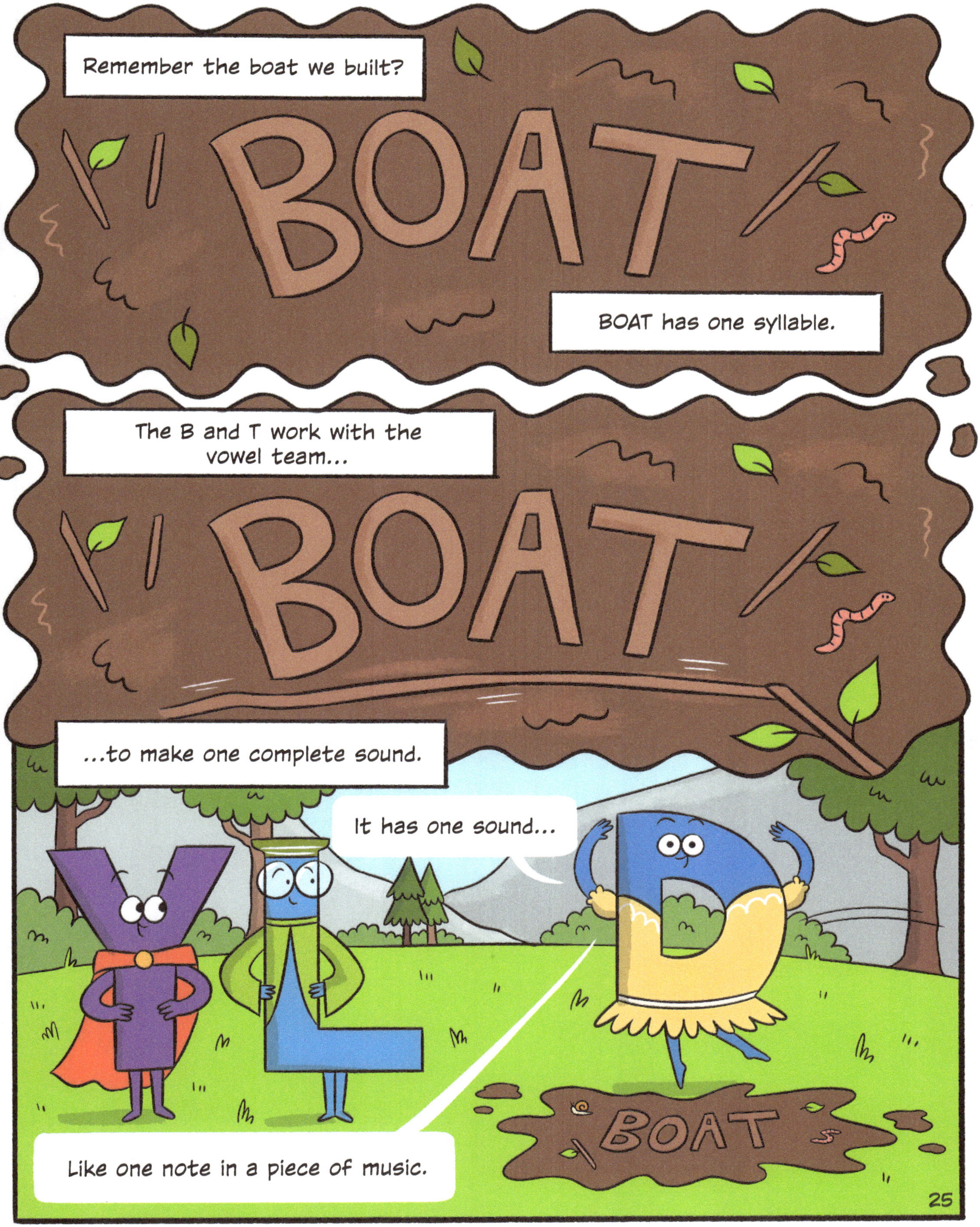

Remember the boat we built?
BOAT
BOAT has one syllable.
The B and T work with the vowel team...
BOAT
...to make one complete sound.
It has one sound...
Like one note in a piece of music.
BOAT

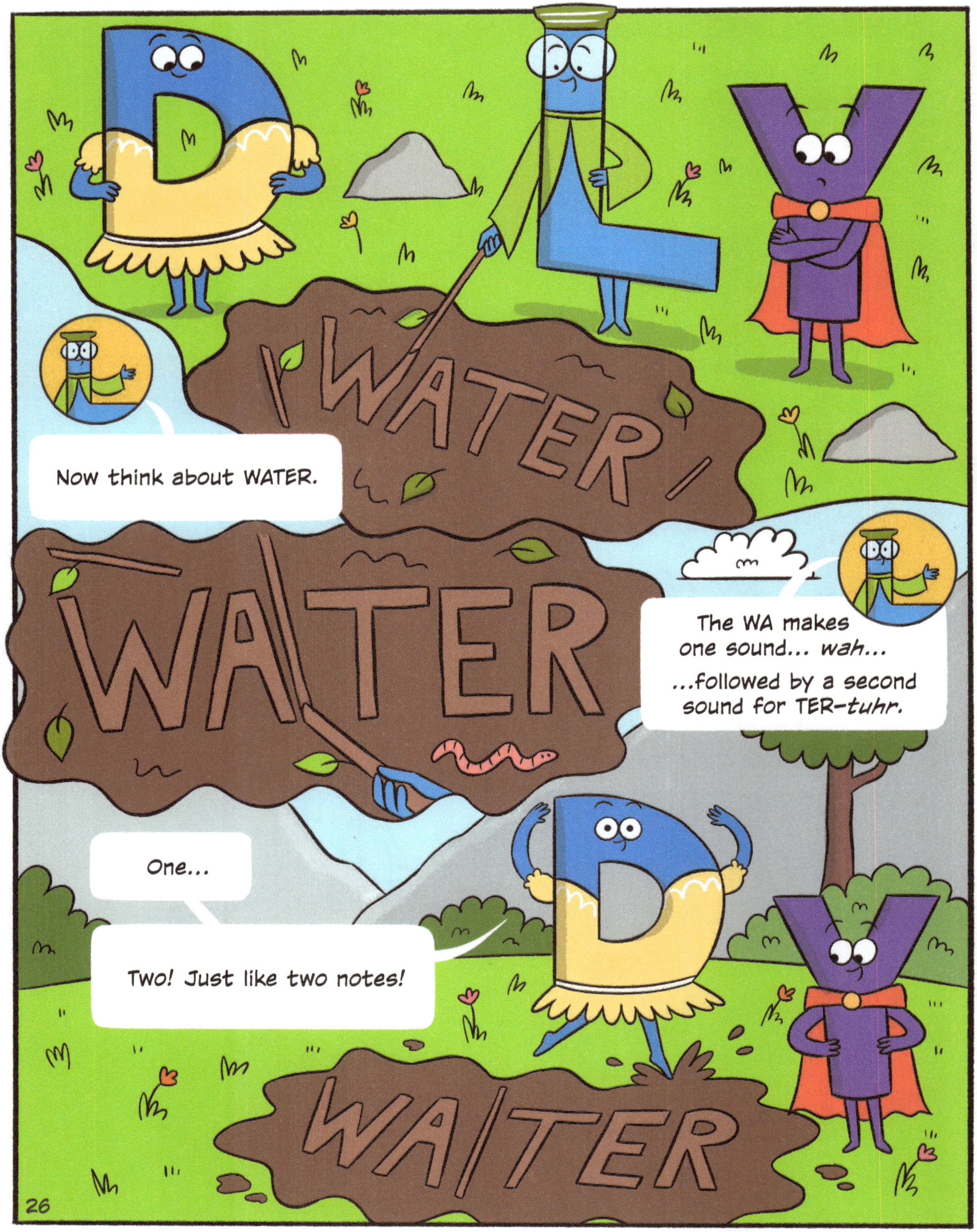
WATER
Now think about WATER.
WA|TER
The WA makes one sound... *wah*...
...followed by a second sound for TER–*tuhr*.
One...
Two! Just like two notes!
WA|TER

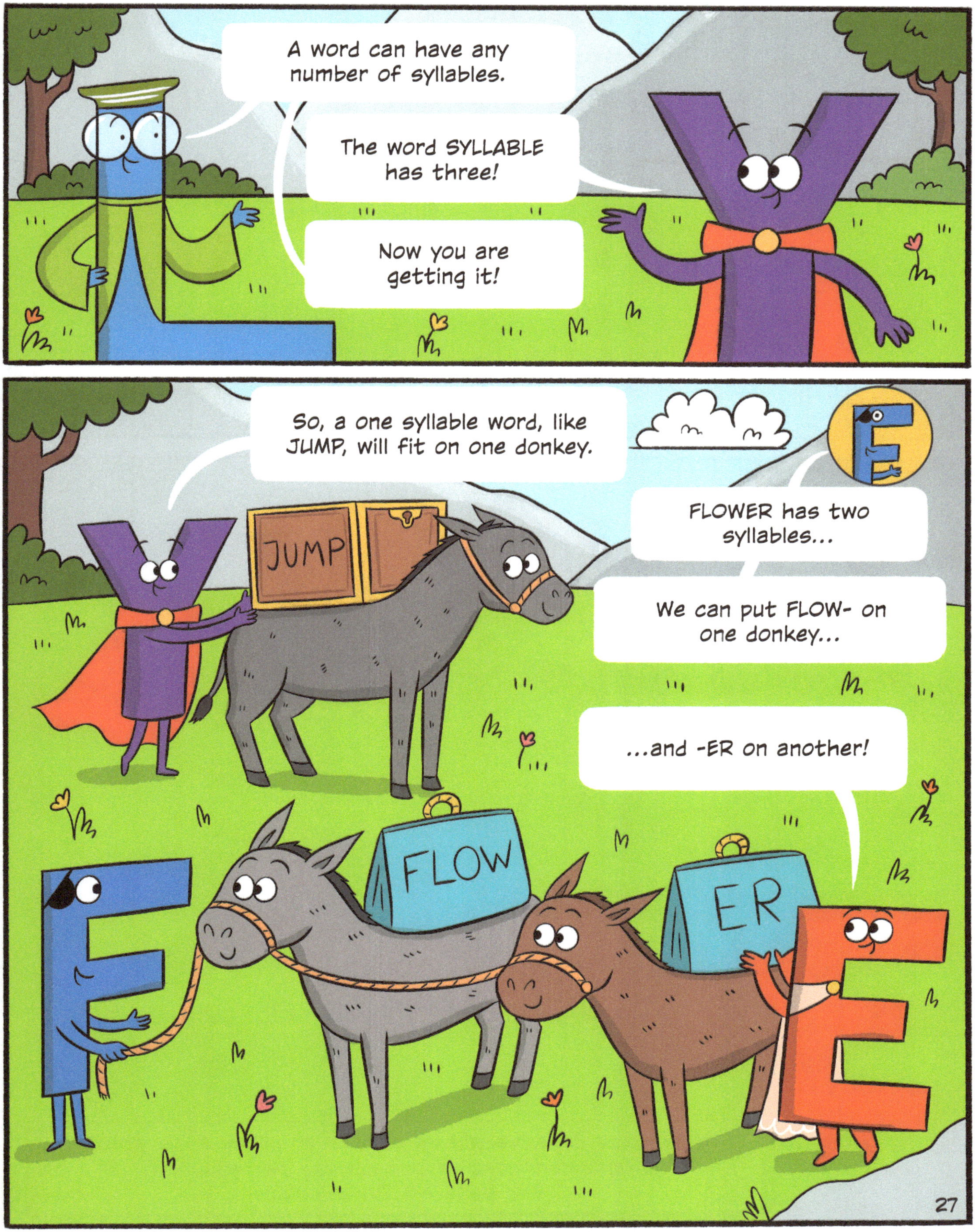
A word can have any number of syllables.
The word SYLLABLE has three!
Now you are getting it!
So, a one syllable word, like JUMP, will fit on one donkey.
JUMP
FLOWER has two syllables...
We can put FLOW- on one donkey...
...and -ER on another!
FLOW
ER

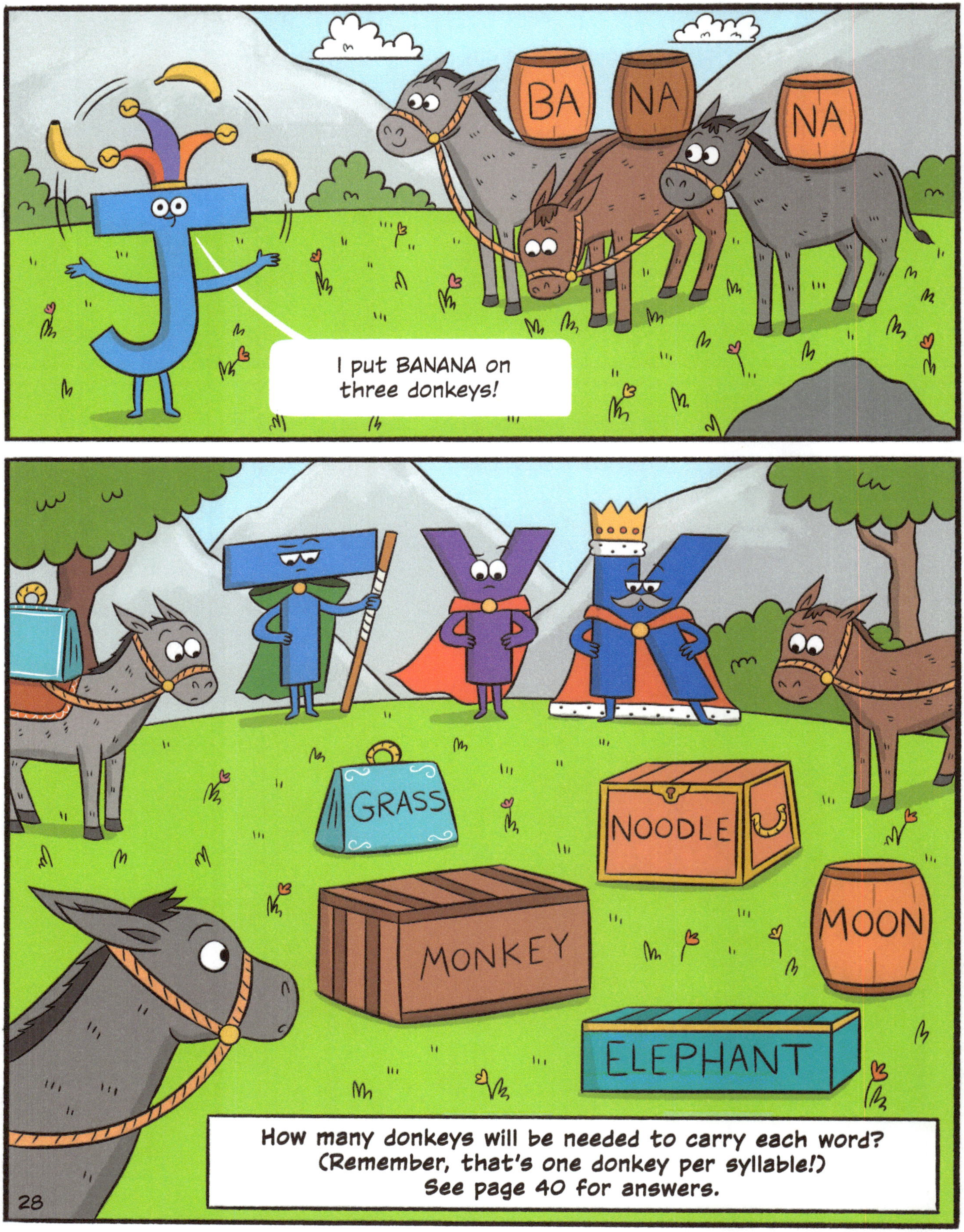
BA
NA
NA
I put BANANA on three donkeys!
GRASS
NOODLE
MONKEY
MOON
ELEPHANT
How many donkeys will be needed to carry each word?
(Remember, that's one donkey per syllable!)
See page 40 for answers.

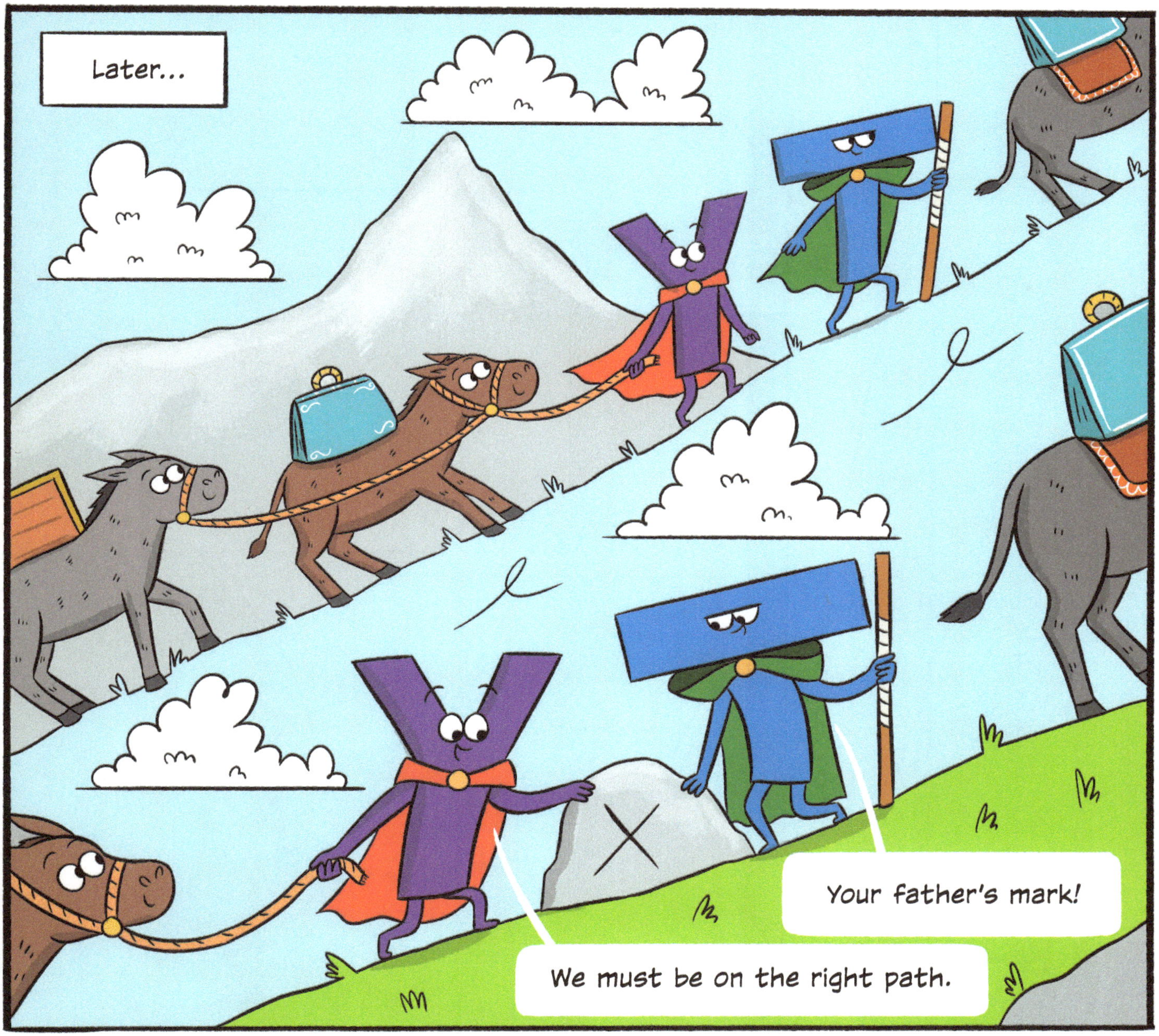
Later...
Your father's mark!
We must be on the right path.

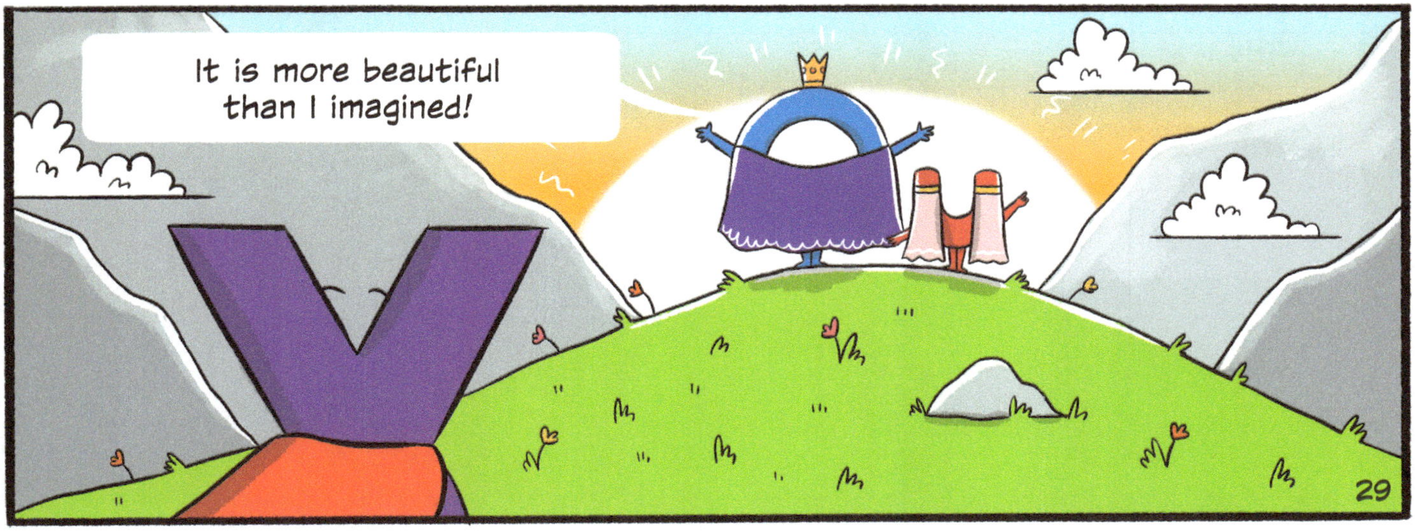
It is more beautiful than I imagined!

SILENT LETTERS

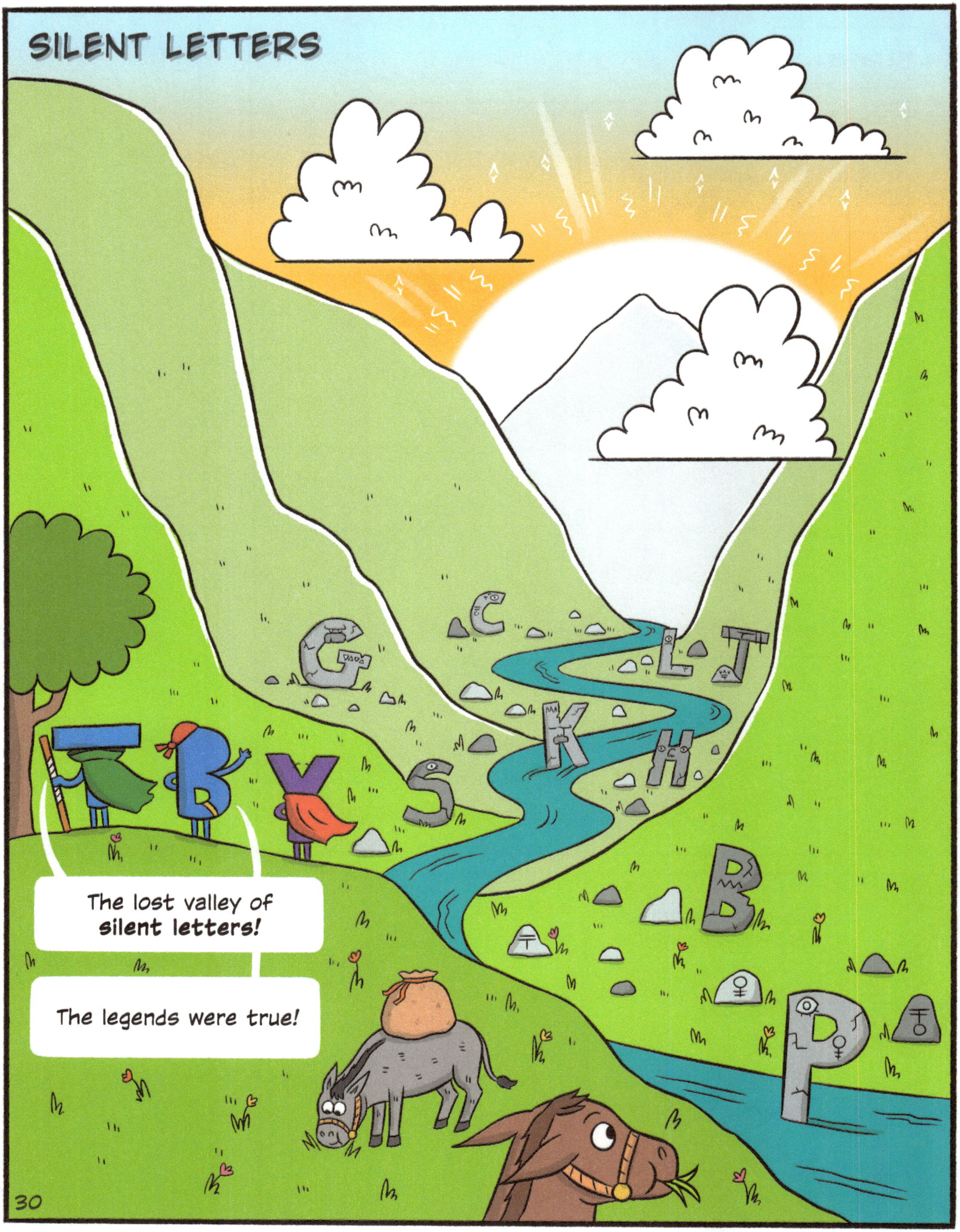
The lost valley of **silent letters!**
The legends were true!

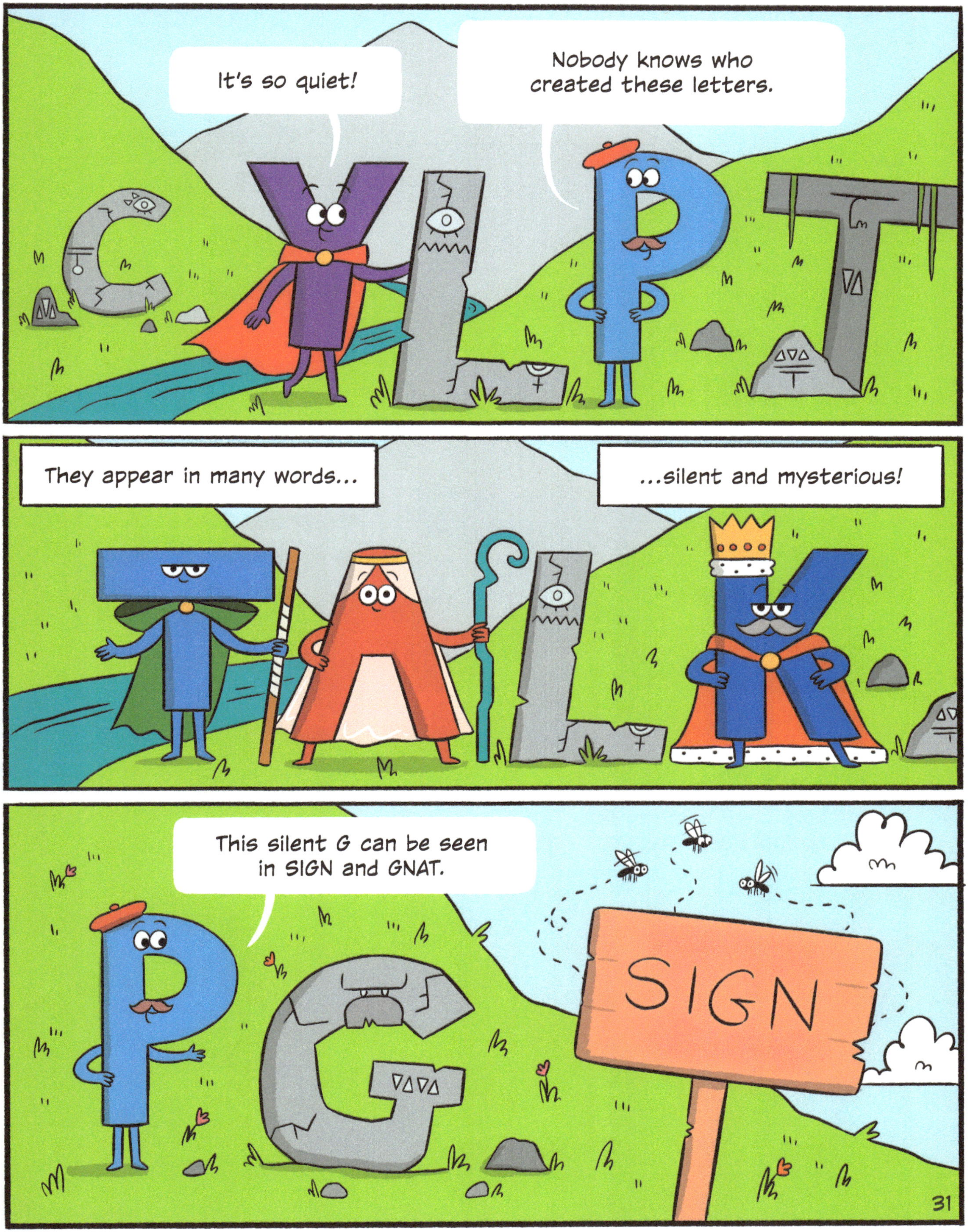

It's so quiet!
Nobody knows who created these letters.
They appear in many words...
...silent and mysterious!
This silent G can be seen in SIGN and GNAT.
SIGN

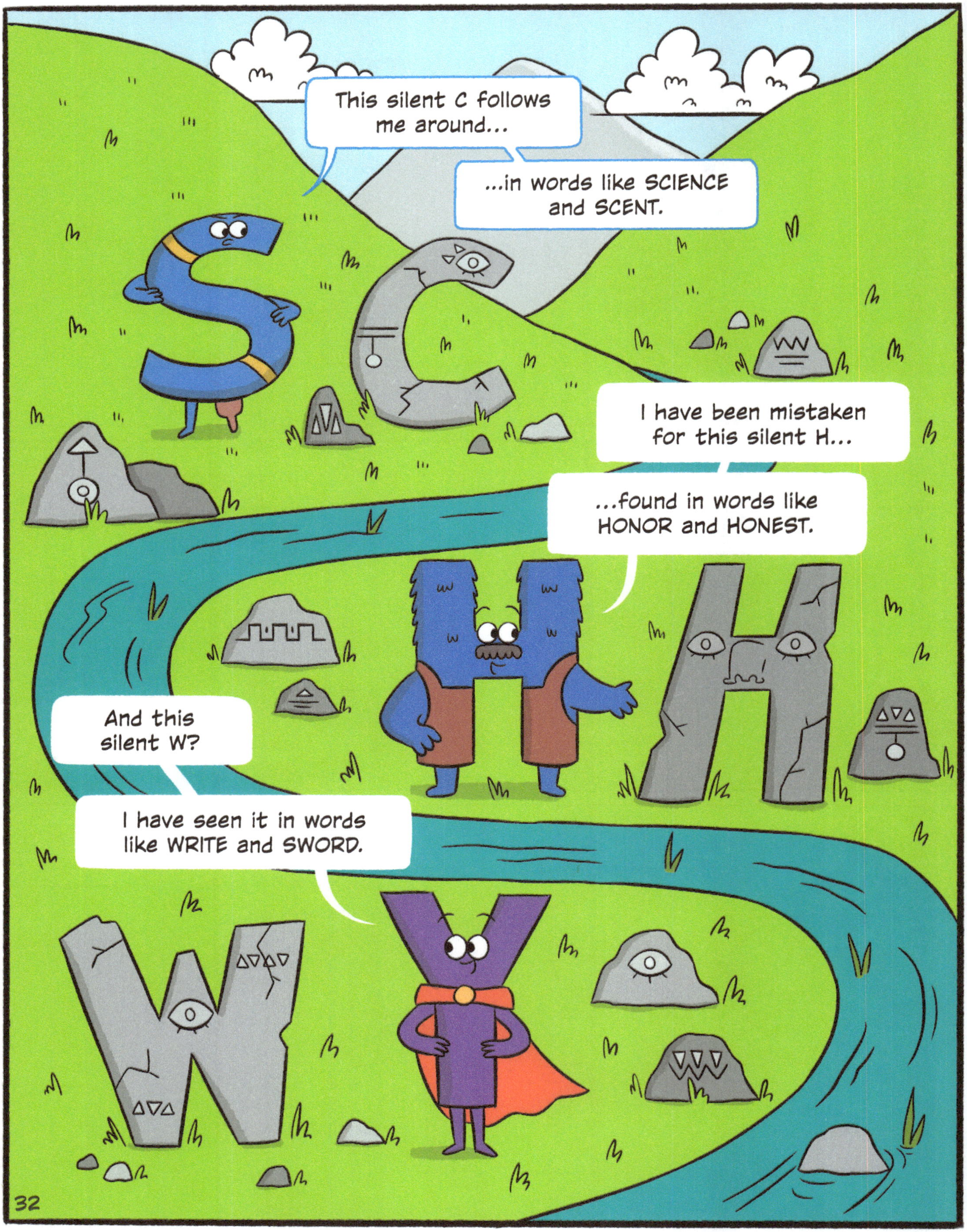
This silent C follows me around...
...in words like SCIENCE and SCENT.
I have been mistaken for this silent H...
...found in words like HONOR and HONEST.
And this silent W?
I have seen it in words like WRITE and SWORD.

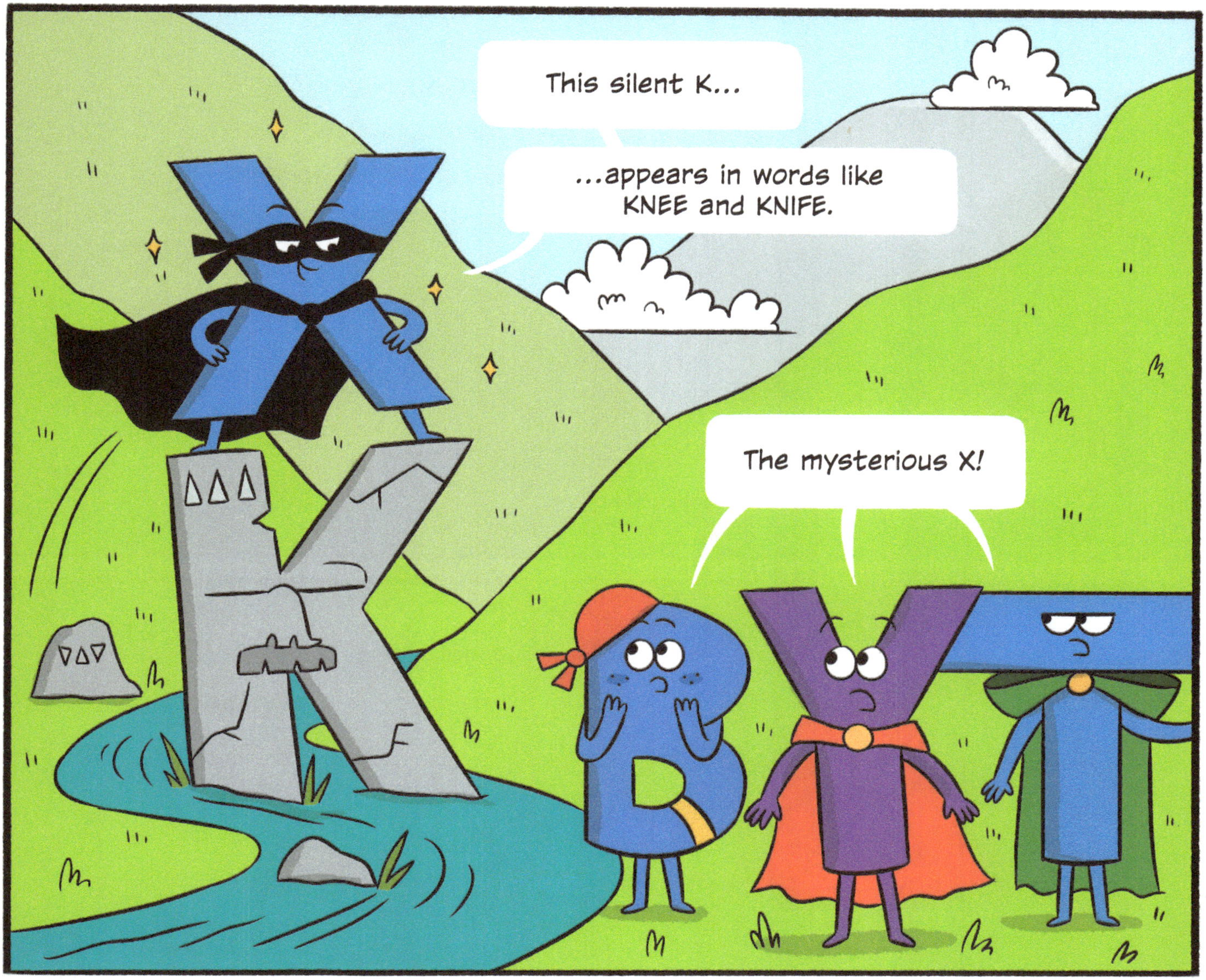
This silent K...
...appears in words like KNEE and KNIFE.
The mysterious X!

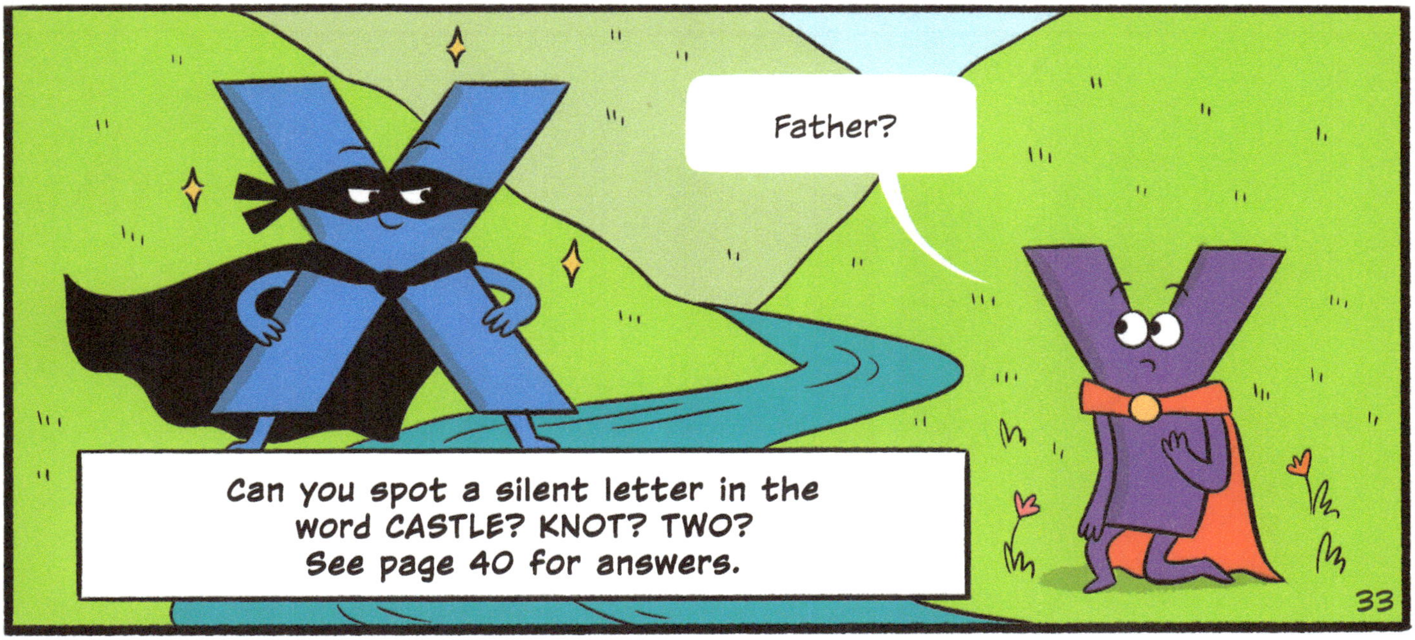
Father?
Can you spot a silent letter in the word CASTLE? KNOT? TWO? See page 40 for answers.

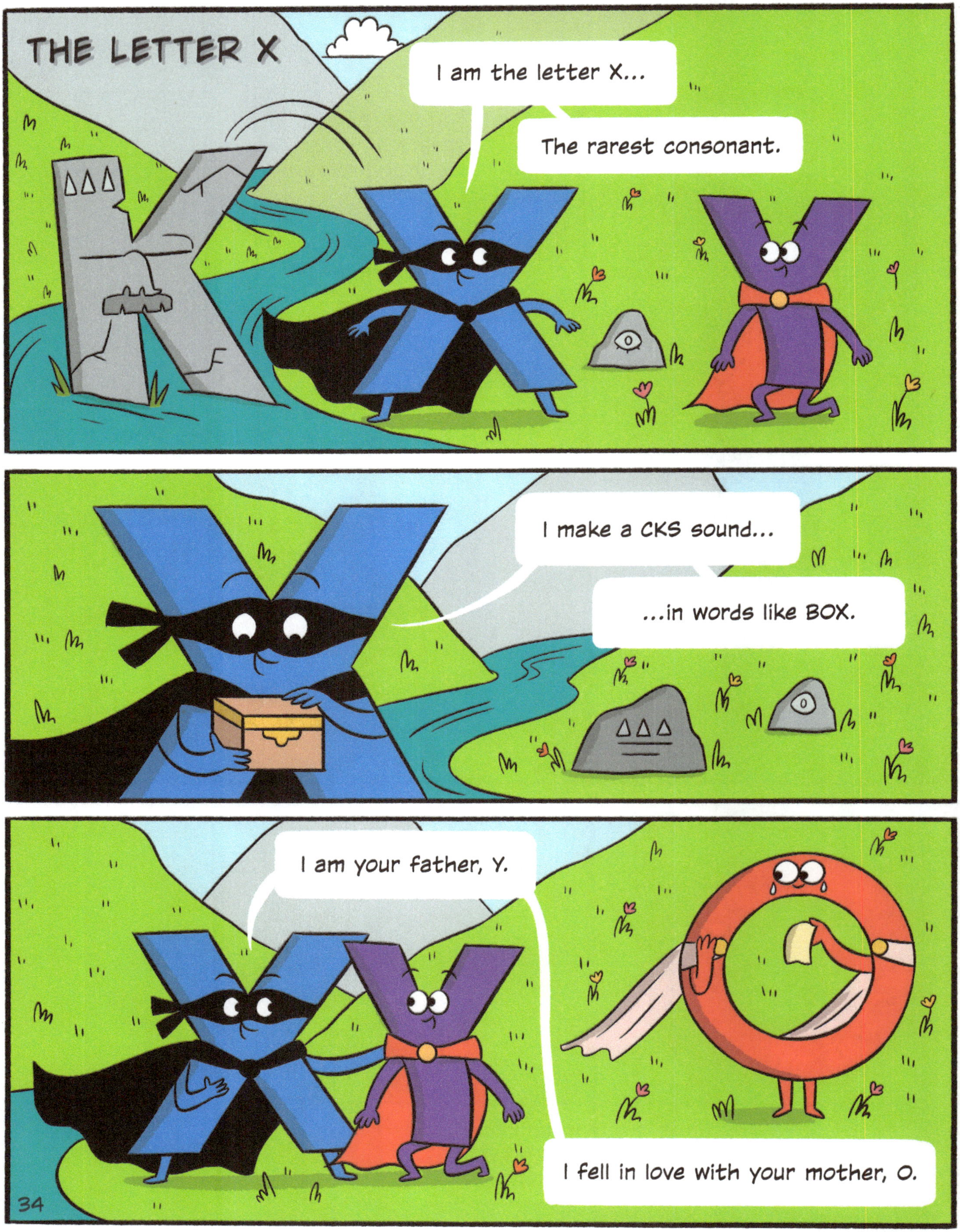
THE LETTER X
I am the letter X...
The rarest consonant.
I make a CKS sound...
...in words like BOX.
I am your father, Y.
I fell in love with your mother, O.

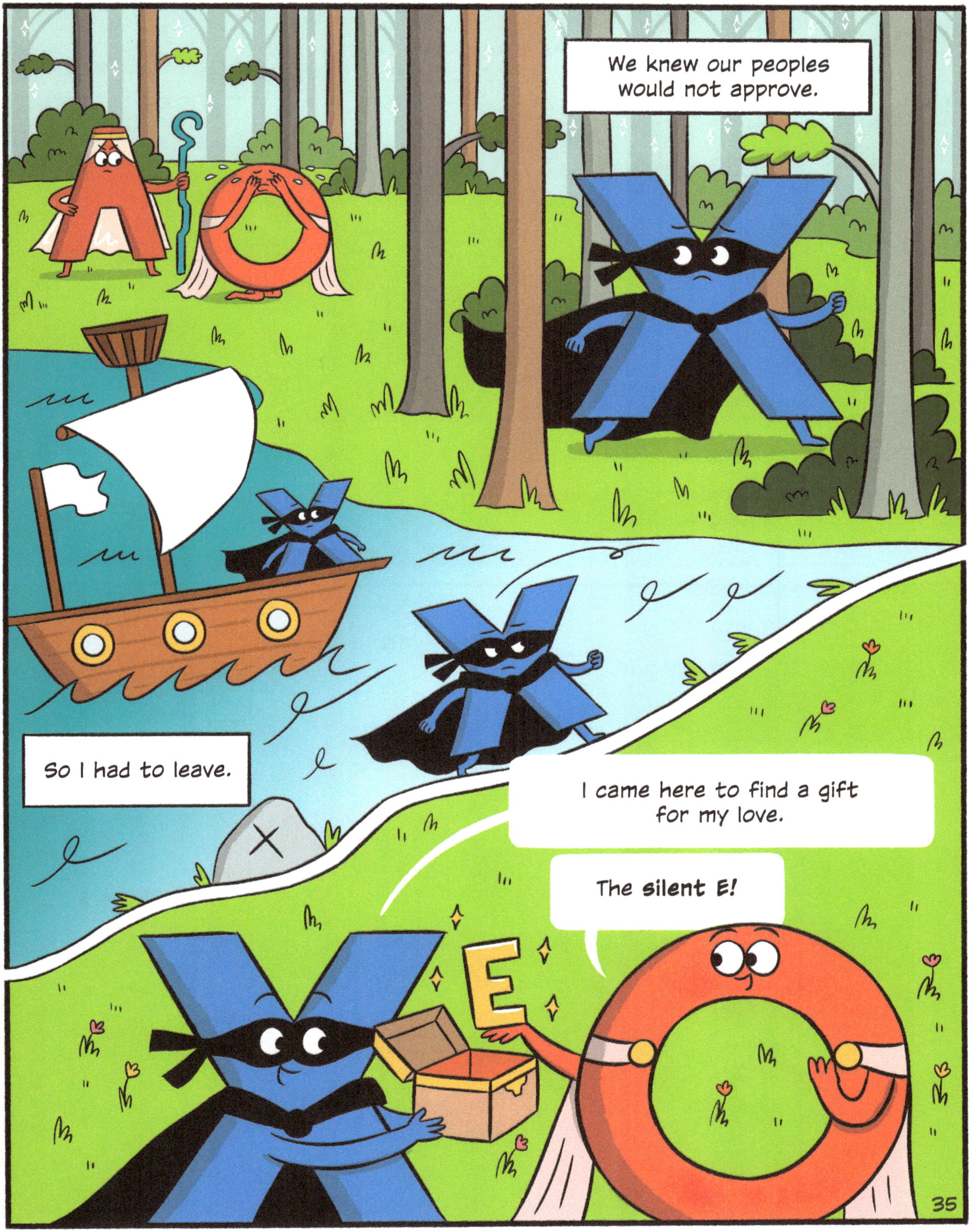

We knew our peoples would not approve.
So I had to leave.
I came here to find a gift for my love.
The **silent E!**
E

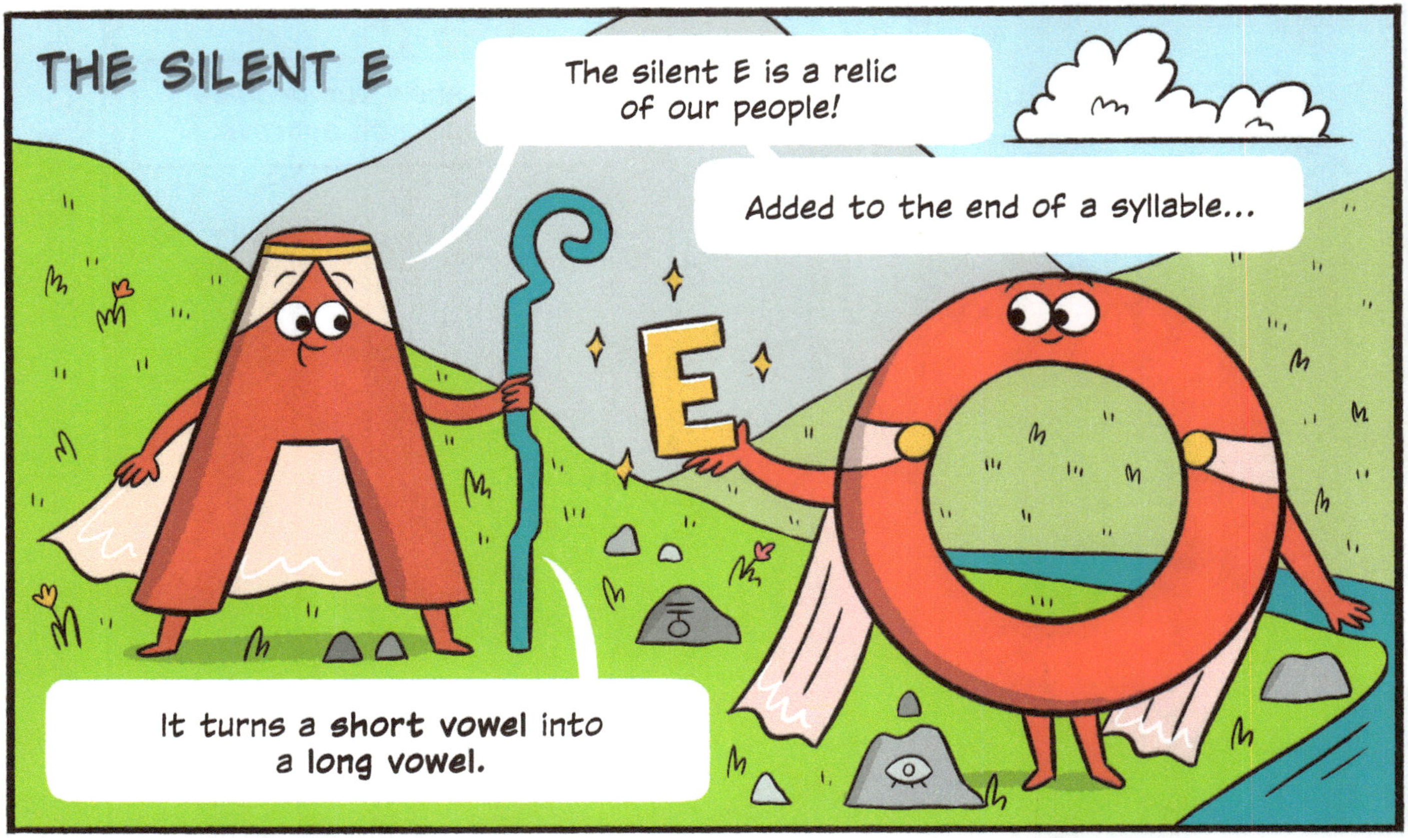
THE SILENT E
The silent E is a relic of our people!
Added to the end of a syllable...
It turns a **short vowel** into a **long vowel**.

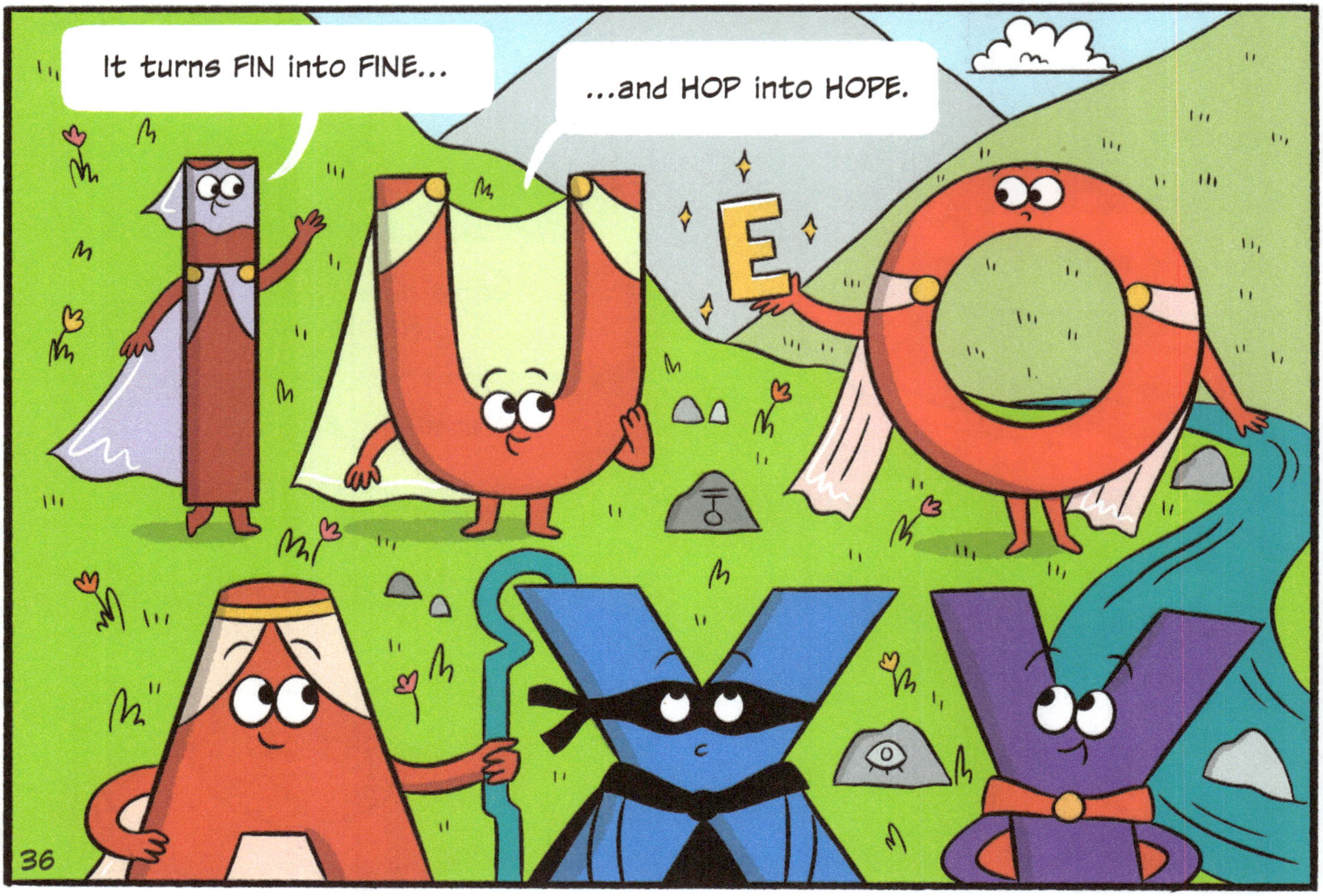
It turns FIN into FINE...
...and HOP into HOPE.

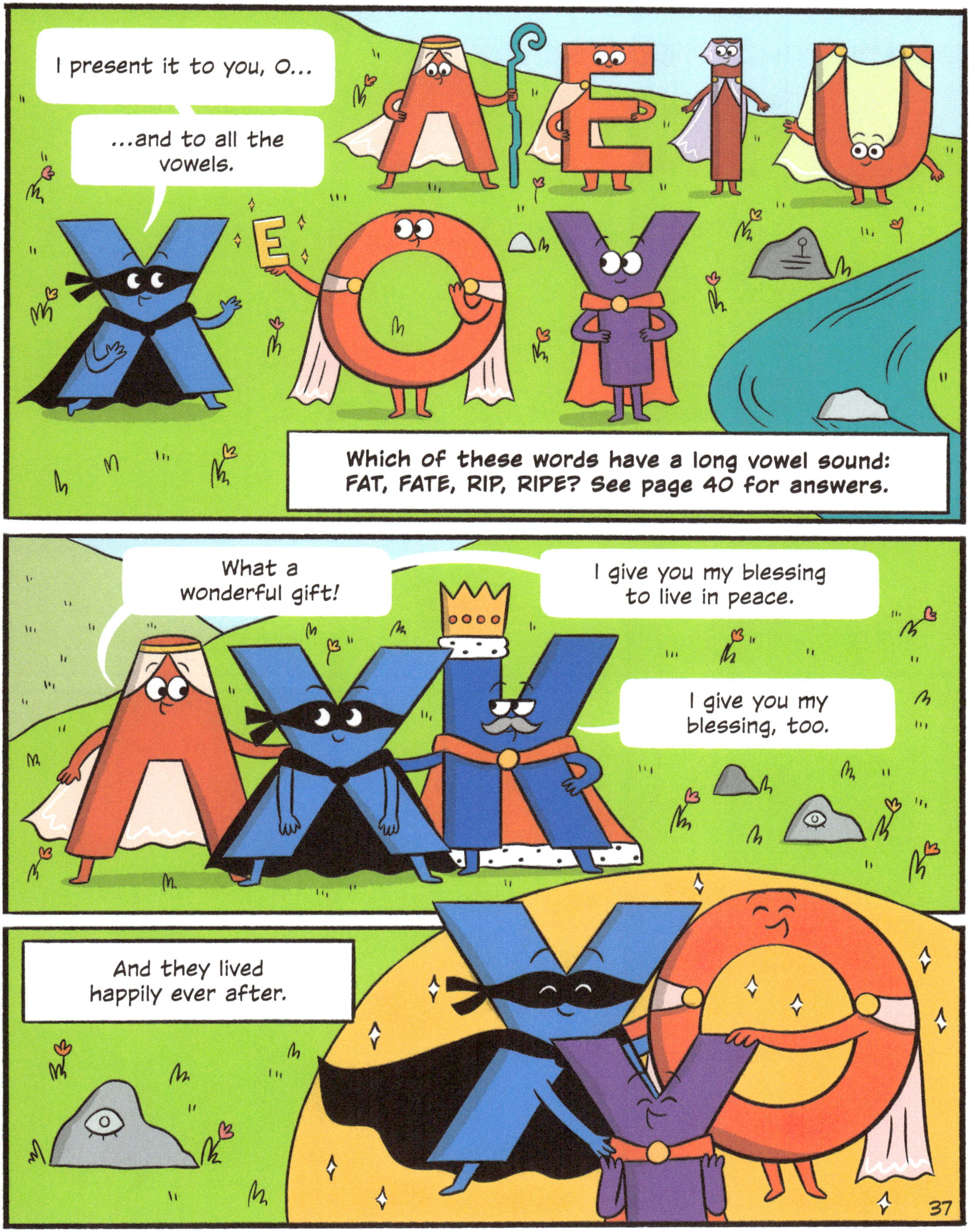
I present it to you, O...
...and to all the vowels.
Which of these words have a long vowel sound: FAT, FATE, RIP, RIPE? See page 40 for answers.
What a wonderful gift!
I give you my blessing to live in peace.
I give you my blessing, too.
And they lived happily ever after.

SHOW WHAT YOU KNOW

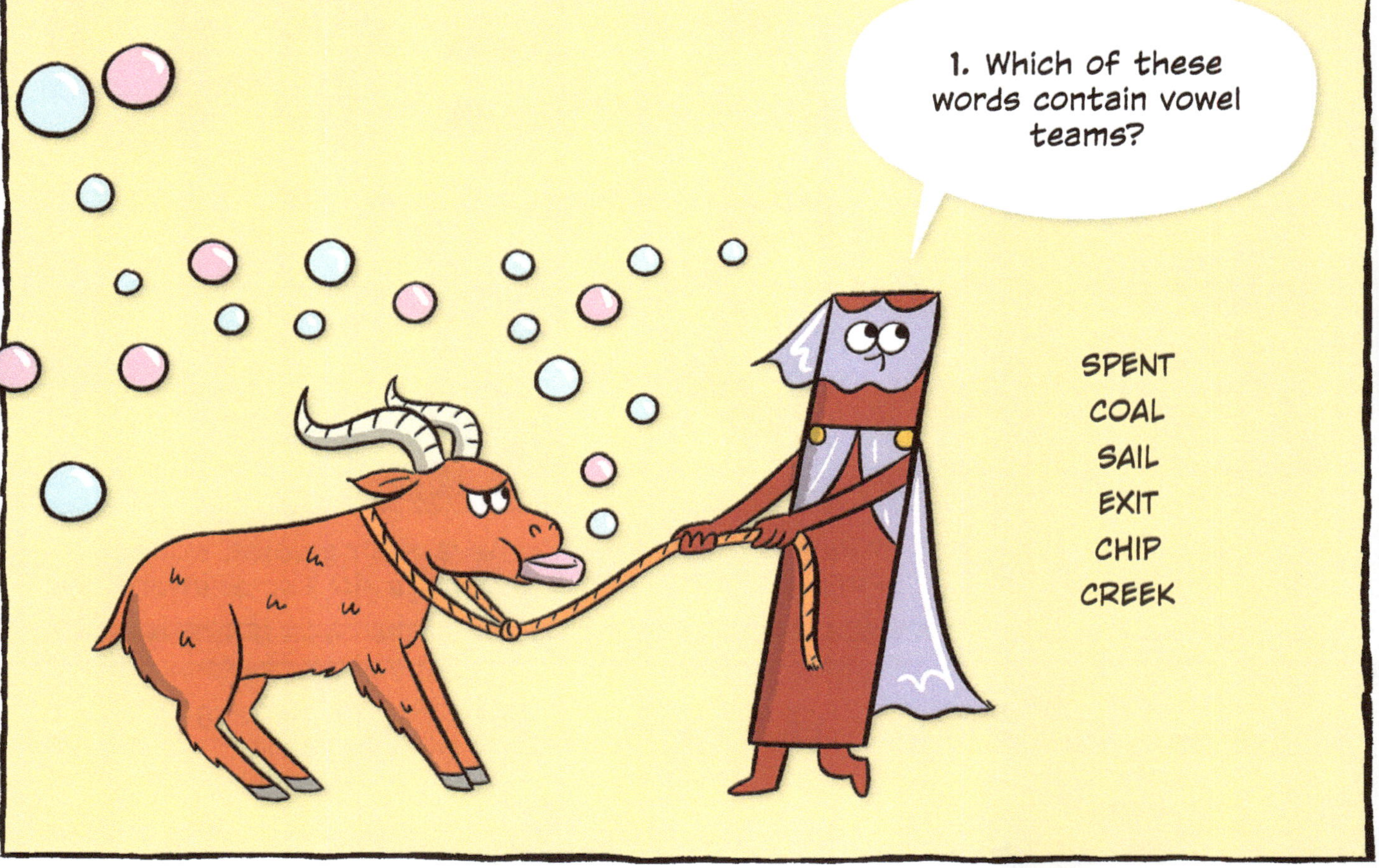

1. Which of these words contain vowel teams?
SPENT
COAL
SAIL
EXIT
CHIP
CREEK

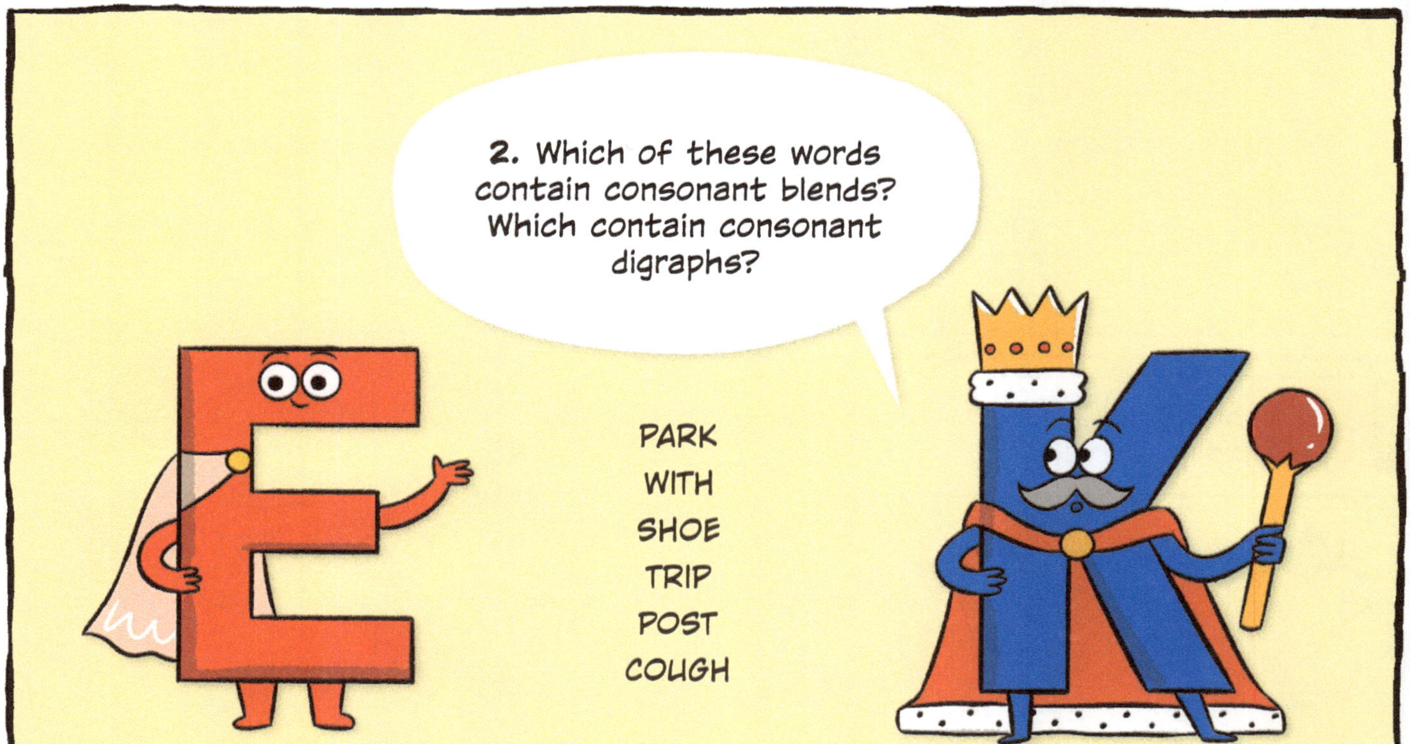

2. Which of these words contain consonant blends? Which contain consonant digraphs?
PARK
WITH
SHOE
TRIP
POST
COUGH

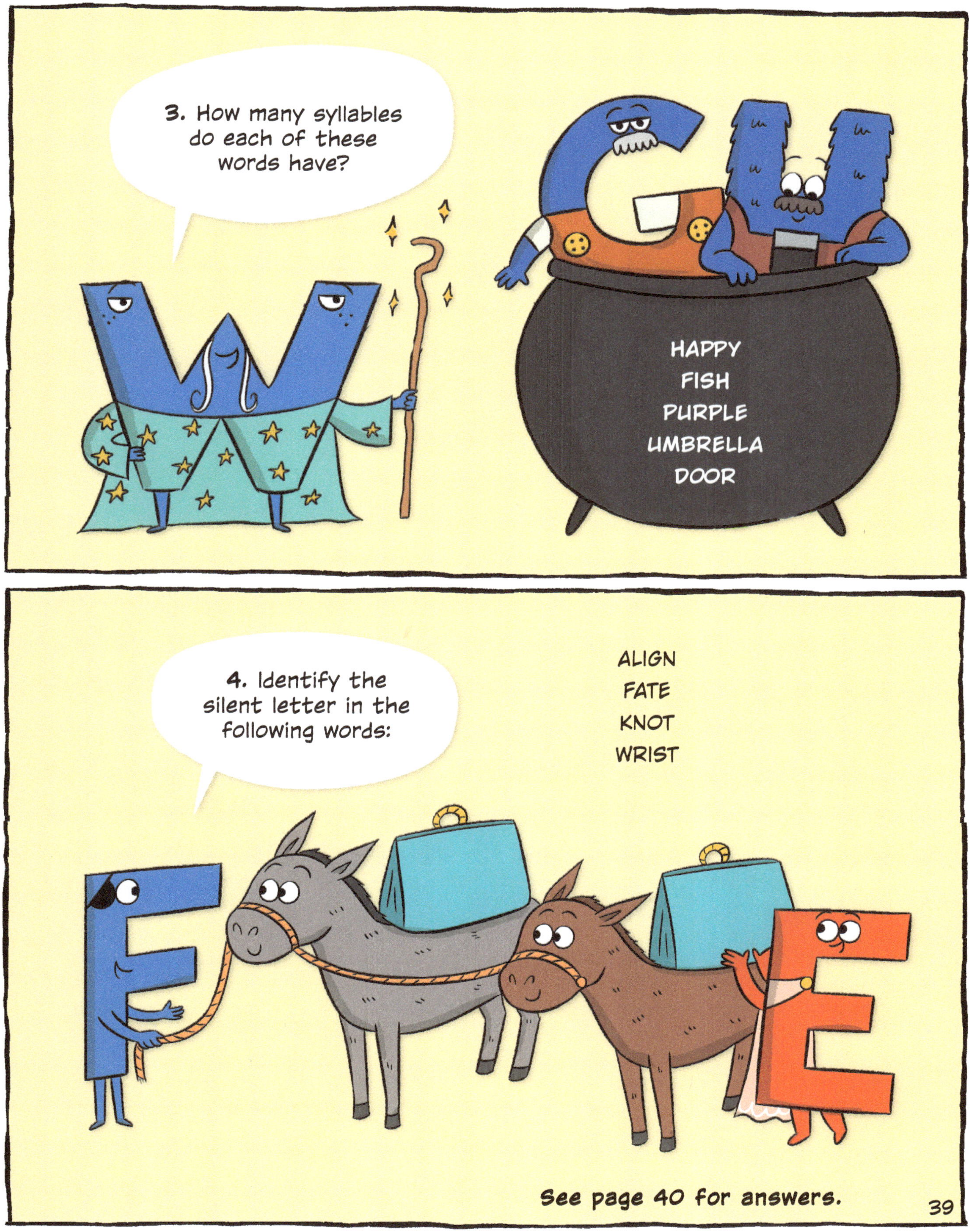
3. How many syllables do each of these words have?
HAPPY
FISH
PURPLE
UMBRELLA
DOOR
4. Identify the silent letter in the following words:
ALIGN
FATE
KNOT
WRIST

See page 40 for answers.

ANSWERS

page 7: CR<u>Y</u>- VOWEL
<u>Y</u>EAR- CONSONANT
<u>Y</u>OU- CONSONANT

page 13: Sail into the B<u>AY</u>.
Land on the B<u>EA</u>CH here.
Watch out for the SN<u>AI</u>L!

page 21: Vowel teams: AI, OU
Consonant blends: PR, ST
Digraphs: CH, TH

page 28: GRASS-1
MONKEY-2
NOODLE-2
MOON-1
ELEPHANT-3

page 33: CAS<u>T</u>LE
<u>K</u>NOT
T<u>W</u>O

page 37: FAT<u>E</u>
RIP<u>E</u>

SHOW WHAT YOU KNOW ANSWERS
pages 38-39:

1. C<u>OA</u>L, S<u>AI</u>L, CR<u>EE</u>K

2. consonant blends: PARK, TRIP, POST
consonant digraphs: WI<u>TH</u>, <u>SH</u>OE, COU<u>GH</u>

3. HAPPY- 2
FISH- 1
PURPLE- 2
UMBRELLA- 3
DOOR- 1

4. AL<u>I</u><u>G</u>N
FAT<u>E</u>
<u>K</u>NOT
<u>W</u>RIST

WORDS TO KNOW

consonant a letter sounded by stopping or slowing the breath with tongue, teeth, or lips

consonant blend a consonant team in which both consonants lend their sound

consonant digraph a consonant team in which the consonants combine to form a new sound

long vowel a vowel whose sound matches its spoken name

short vowel a vowel whose sound does not match its spoken name

silent E an unpronounced E that turns a vowel long when added to the end of a syllable

silent letter a letter in a spelled word that is not pronounced

syllable a word or part of a word pronounced as a single unit

vowel a letter with an open sound, in which the breath flows freely

vowel team multiple vowels working together to make a single sound